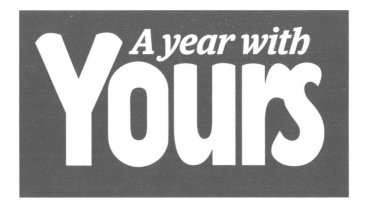

Name	
Address	
Postcode	
Home phone	
Mobile phone	
Email	

In case of emergency, contact:

Name	
Telephone	

D1355729

USEFUL CONTACTS

BANK	
BUILDING SOCIETY	
CHEMIST/PHARMACY	
CHIROPODIST	
COUNCIL	
CREDIT CARD EMERGENCY	
DENTIST	
DOCTOR	
ELECTRICIAN	
GARAGE	
HAIRDRESSER	
HOSPITAL	
LOCAL POLICE	
MILKMAN	
OPTICIAN	
PLUMBER	
SOLICITOR	
TAXI	
VET	

RENEWAL REMINDERS

	RENEWAL DATE	POLICY NUMBER	TELEPHONE
CAR INSURANCE			
CAR TAX			
MOT			
HOME INSURANCE			
TV LICENCE			
PET INSURANCE			
Yours SUBSCRIPTION			

THE YEAR AHEAD

Put a spring in

BATHE IN BLUEBELLS

Ashridge Estate, Berkhamstead, Hertfordshire

To witness a sea of beautiful bluebells head to the Ashridge Estate in Hertfordshire, where swathes of these delicate flowers lie peacefully under the canopy of the trees. They are normally in bloom in May and weekends are busy so try to visit on a weekday, if possible. The best way to explore the estate is by foot or by bike as there are miles of footpaths and bridleways to investigate. Call into the visitor centre on arrival and they'll provide you with a map, guiding you to the bluebells.
www.nationaltrust.org.uk/ashridge-estate

DAFFODIL WALK

Farndale, North Yorkshire Moors National Park

During mid-March and mid-April take a walk in the area famously known as the 'daffodil dale'. Stroll through the Yorkshire Moors and be flanked by wild daffodils as you meander along the riverbank and through fields. The most straightforward route is a three-and-half-mile walk alongside the River Dove, from Low Mill to Church Houses and back. For some light refreshments call into the aptly named Daffy Café for a cup of tea and a scone.
www.real-whitby.co.uk/farndale-daffodil-walk

RIVER RAMBLE

Lynmouth to Watersmeet, Exmoor, Devon

After their winter hibernation, our river valleys spring back into life as leaves bud, wildflowers sway in the breeze, and the sunlight penetrates the water. The best place to enjoy this is in one of Britain's deepest river gorges where the East Lyn River and Hoar Oak Water meet. Take the Coleridge Way east to Watersmeet and then branch south to Hillsford Bridge returning along the Tarka Trail high up above the woodland on the south side of the valley and you'll be rewarded with a spectacular view over the Bristol Channel.
www.nationaltrust.org.uk/watersmeet

your step!

A WALK IN THE FOREST

Lyndhurst to Beaulieu River, New Forest
The New Forest is a beautiful mix of ancient woods and vast heathlands. With nearly 150 miles of public footpaths to choose from you'll be spoilt for choice. The historic town of Lyndhurst makes a good starting point, with several circular routes from Bolton's Bench, just south of town. Keep your eyes open as you're likely to spot New Forest ponies and wild pigs - you may even be lucky enough to catch a glimpse of a roe or fallow deer.
www.thenewforest.co.uk

BEAUTIFUL BLOSSOMS

Lenham village, Kent
With its acres of apple and cherry orchards Kent is known as the fruit belt of England. The best time of year to enjoy this landscape is in spring when the area bursts into bloom and glorious apple and cherry trees are coated in glorious blossom. Many of the best walks in this area can include a stroll through Kent's community orchards, such as Sheldwich on the edge of the Downs, Stockbury, high on the Downs, and Lenham, Milstead and Lynsted.
www.kentdowns.org.uk

MOUNTAIN VIEW

Craflwyn, Snowdonia
You don't need to be an expert climber to enjoy Snowdonia, there are plenty of walks around the area if you don't fancy climbing up a mountain. This riverside walk will take you through ancient landscapes full of history and legends. There's plenty of beautiful spring colour to see. Keep an eye out for wildflowers such as: hay rattle, purple loosestrife, whorled caraway and ragged robin.
www.nationaltrust.org.uk/ craflwyn-and-beddgelert

COMB THE COAST

Three Cliffs Bay, Gower Peninsula, Wales
The Gower Peninsula is regularly billed as 'Britain's Best Beach' or 'Best View' and was designated the UK's first Area of Outstanding Natural Beauty (AONB) in 1956. The best time to visit this popular area is spring,

before the crowds descend in high summer. You'll find plenty to keep you entertained on this varied shoreline of sand dunes, salt marshes and signature limestone cliffs. Enjoy a spot of history by visiting the Neolithic Giant's Grave and the ruins of 13th-century Pennard Castle.
www.explore-gower.co.uk

7

Superb succulents

Fiona Cumberpatch introduces us to some quirky plants that are inexpensive, easy to look after and are almost indestructible!

With their funky shapes, interesting textures and vibrant colours, these versatile plants are having a fashionable moment - and for good reason. Their clean lines and defined shapes look stunning when planted in copper or galvanised steel containers, or used more naturally among pebbles and gravel.

Originating from warm, dry areas, including the Mediterranean, Mexico and Africa, where they thrive in poor soil, succulents are perfect for gardeners who don't have much time as they don't need special care and shrug off most pests. Their thick, fleshy leaves and stems store water, so they rarely require watering either. Although they do flower, they are especially prized for their foliage which comes in geometric shapes and an array of colours, from cool greens to glowing reds, warm golds and deep, rich purples in all shapes and sizes.

HOW TO PLANT

Succulents are happiest and look especially striking grouped in pots and planters. The pots you choose must have drainage holes in the bottom as these plants dislike having wet roots. They need to be planted in a specialist cactus compost which has a gritty texture and contains the nutrients and trace elements these plants need. Once your plants are established, re-pot them in late spring if they have outgrown their container. And don't worry about disturbing them - they're tough customers and won't mind being moved.

LOOKING AFTER THEM

During the spring and summer, allow the plants' compost to dry out between watering rather than keeping it constantly moist. If you give them too much water, they will start to rot. Watering once every two weeks is a good rule. Succulents need to grow in full sun. They thrive on warmth, which helps to develop the colours of their foliage. A three-weekly summer feed, using an all-purpose liquid feed, will make their colours even deeper and richer, but it's not essential as they'll do well enough without it. If you see any mouldy or dead leaves, gently remove them. If dust builds up in the spaces between their intricate leaves, use a thin, soft paintbrush to brush it away. Wipe smooth leaves gently with a damp cloth to keep them looking glossy and bright.

During the winter months, succulents may need to be wrapped up to protect them against harsh frosts – bubble wrap or horticultural fleece is ideal for this. If you can, bring them inside or stand them in a sheltered porch until the weather warms up. If plants look dead, especially after the winter, give them at least three months before you throw them away. They may well surprise you by coming back to life!

Modern Gardens, hundreds of easy ideas, projects and fresh inspiration every month!

3 OF THE BEST

Aloe vera
Dense clumps of spiky light green leaves proudly display soft 'teeth' along the edges. They provide texture, sculpture and height.
Height 35-100cm (13-39in) Spread 30cm (12in)

'Black rose'
The glossy dark purple rosette leaves of this plant, also known as Aeonium 'Zwartkop', have bright lime-green centres, adding colour and depth in a mixed pot - or you can grow it alone for a dramatic feature. It will need bringing inside or protecting during the winter, especially if you live in a colder part of the UK.
Height 1-1.5m (39-60in) Spread 1-1.5m (39-60in)

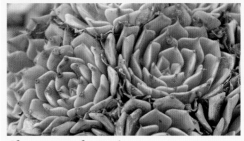

Glaucous echeveria
Featuring silvery-green-grey leaves and dramatic pink and yellow spines of flowers, it's hardy enough to withstand British winters outdoors when protected from frost next to a wall. It spreads by forming new rosettes.
Height and spread: Up to 50cm (20in)

Best of British

GREAT SCOT

It's not just the countryside that looks radiant in the spring – some of the UK's cities look just as pretty. Edinburgh is one of them, thanks to parks lined with cherry blossom, and hillsides which catch the spring sunlight. Miss out the mania of the August Fringe Festival, and instead enjoy quiet open spaces, such as the 70-acre Royal Botanic Garden. If you get caught in an April shower (no matter the month) you can shelter in the Victorian Palm House – the tallest in Britain. Fans of flowers will also enjoy Dunbars Close Garden – a hidden gem on the Royal Mile – which is packed with flowers and fruit trees, and free to explore. It was designed to look like a 17th century garden, despite being planted in 1976.
Royal Botanic Garden is free, glasshouse is £5.50 adults, free for children. Call 01312 482909 or visit www.rbge.org.uk

Did you know?
The UK is home to nearly half of the world's population of our native bluebell (Hyacinthoides non-scripta)

TRY SOMETHING NEW...

At this time of year, your garden will be teeming with feathery friends, all looking to mate and rear chicks – so if you've ever considered bird watching, now's the time to do it. A study from the University of Exeter found that people who regularly watch birds were less likely to suffer from depression, anxiety and stress, so a spot of twitching could be just what the doctor ordered! For lots of free tips on identifying birds, **Visit www.rspb.org.uk/birds-and-wildlife/read-and-learn/watching-birds/**

DON'T BE BLUE

In our opinion, there's no fragrance as intoxicating as the heady perfume of native bluebells. These purple-tinged beauties are always a welcome sight after a long winter, and wandering the gardens at the Blickling Estate in Norfolk is sure to raise your spirits. Follow the carpet of flowers through the historic oak woodland and breathe deeply! The handsome redbrick house itself is also worth a visit, especially if you're keen on art, as it's home to paintings by Gainsborough and many others. Plus, if you visit on the Easter weekend you're more than likely to find a chocolate egg hunt in progress.
Call 01263 738030 or visit www.nationaltrust.org.uk /blickling-estate

PIC: NATIONAL TRUST

PIC: VISIT CHESTER AND CHESHIRE

EAT SEASONALLY

The end of April marks asparagus season, and this yummy veg is grown in abundance in Cheshire. Consider a foodie pilgrimage through its various market towns, including Medieval Nantwich and lively Knutsford for independent shops to tickle your taste buds. As well as asparagus, the county is famed for its apples, gooseberries and cheeses. Organised tours of local food producers can be arranged, including a flour mill, organic farm shops and an apple orchard,
Book a bespoke Cheshire tour (prices vary) at http://gourmetfoodtrails.com

LAMB-TASTIC!

Along with Easter bunnies and flowers, nothing says 'spring' quite like the sight of newly-born lambs leaping around in fields. The valleys of the Brecon Beacons are perfect for spotting little woolly bundles – you might be lucky enough to witness a birth – as well as being stunning in their own right. The Upper Tarell Valley, South Wales, is filled with semi-ancient woodlands and surrounded by wild mountains. One of the most heartening sights in the Coed Carno and Coed Herbert woods are the 'phoenix' trees which have fallen, but continue to grow anyway, adding a green canopy to the forest floor. Look out for pied flycatchers, redstart, bluebells, red campion and all sorts of other natural wonders.

THREE OF THE BEST...

...blooming woodlands
Greet the new shoots, unfurling leaves and frisky birds and animals with a day out in one of the UK's most glorious green spaces.

◆ Glen Finglas in Stirling is a whopper of an ancient wood, covering more than 10,000 acres (albeit slightly fragmented.) As well as being wonderfully evocative thanks to its waterfalls, hills and resident deer, it also offers good disabled access from paths out of the car park opposite Lendrick Lodge.

◆ It's not a wild woodland, but the Brogdale Collections in Kent are a wonderful way to enjoy fruit trees at their blossomy best. The orchards, which constitute the National Fruit Collection, contain apples, pears, cherries, plums, quince, nuts, currants and medlars – many of which will have burst into flower come spring. Follow a guided or self-guided tour.
Tickets £12 adults, £5.50 children. Call 01795 536250 or visit ◆ For a grand entrance, visit

PIC: NATIONAL TRUST

Clumber Park in Nottinghamshire, where a three-mile avenue of 170-year-old lime trees greet you. Here you'll find 170 tree species, including 13 types of oak, as well as roe and fallow deer who live on the grounds.
Tickets cost £3.85 adults, £1.95 children. Visit www.nationaltrust.org.uk/clumber-park

Bunny basket

This cute crocheted bag is ideal for Easter egg hunts!

YOU WILL NEED

100g (3oz) of Sirdar Cotton Rich Aran Cream (MC)
50g (2oz) of Sirdar Cotton Rich Aran Blush (CC)
Black yarn for eyes
4.5mm and 6mm crochet hooks
Yarn sewing up needle
Toy stuffing

ABBREVIATIONS

CH – chain; st(s) - stitch(es); sk – skip; SS – slip stitch; dc – double crochet; htr – half treble; DC2tog – double crochet two together; cm – centimetre(s); cont continue(ing); mm – millimetre(s); g – grams; in – inch(es); rep-repeat(s)(ing)

MAIN BASKET

Round 1: Using 2 strands (MC) with 6mm hook - slip knot then 2 CH st(s).
In 2nd CH work 6xHTRs then SS into 1st to join a ring. 6 st(s)
Round 2: CH 2 DC. 2xDCs into following st(s). SS join 1st. 12 st(s)
Round 3: CH 2 DC. 2xDCs into following st(s) SS join 1st st. 24 st(s)
Round 4: CH 2. 2xDCs into next st, *then a single DC. 2xDCs into next st* rep * to * all the way round. End on 2xDC. 36 st(s).
Round 5: CH 2 then single DC next st. 2xDC's, *then a single DC into the next 2 st(s), followed by 2xDCs into the next * rep * to * round. 48 st(s)
Round 6-16: Work 11 rows in straight rounds without increasing. 48 st(s).
CH 2 SS each row.

THE EARS

Row 1: Choose st off the centre front. Using the front loops pull through a (CC) strand. With 4.5mm hook DC 4 st(s) (front loops only). Turn.
Row 2: CH 2 DC next 3 st(s). 4 st(s)
Row 3: As Row 2.
Row 4: CH 2. DC into 1st st to increase. Rep 3 st(s). 5 st(s)
Row 5: CH 2. DC into 4 st(s). 5 st(s)
Row 6: As Row 5.
Row 7: CH 2. DC into 1st st. Rep 4. 6 st(s)
Row 8: CH 2. DC 5 st(s). 6 st(s)
Rows 9-15: As Row 8.
Row 16: CH 2, SK 1. DC 3 st(s). 4st(s)
Row 17: CH 2, SK 1. DC next st. 3st(s) Break off yarn. Work a row DCs around the ear using (MC) and 4.5mm hook. Finish at rim. Leave 9 unworked st(s) between the ears then rep.

STRAP

Row 1: Pull ear forward. Work back loops. Use 2 strands (MC) and 6mm hook. Pull through CH 2. HTR into 3 st(s). Turn.
Row 2: CH 2. HTR and rep for 3 st(s). 4 st(s).
Rows 3-50: CH 2. Work a HTR into the next 3 st(s). 4 st(s). Break off. Leaving 8 st(s)at the sides sew between front-back strap. Rep behind other ear. Tack with (CC).

THE NOSE

Round 1: Use 1 strand of (CC) and 4.5mm crochet hook, CH 2. Work 6xDCs into 2nd CH from the hook, SS first to join. 6 st(s)
Round 2: CH 2 DC each. SS. 6 st(s) Stuff.
Round 3: CH 2 DC 2tog x3 SS. 3 st(s) Break off and sew. Sew nose on centre.

CHEEKS

Round 1: Using 1 strand of (MC) and 4.5mm hook, CH 2. Work 6xDCs into 2nd CH from hook, SS into first st. 6 st(s)
Round 2: CH 2, then DC. 2xDCs following st(s), SS to join first. 12 st(s)
Round 3: CH 2 DC each. SS to join. 12 st(s)
Round 4: As round 3. 12 st(s)
Round 5: CH 2 then DC2tog 6 times. SS to join. 6 st(s) Stuff.
Round 6: CH 2 then DC2tog 3 times. SS to join. 3 st(s) Break off and sew up. Sew cheeks under the nose.

EYES

Embroider eyes using black wool.

Project taken from Hobbycraft

Beaches & birds

BRACING CLIFF WALK

Seaford to Eastbourne, Seven Sisters, East Sussex

This classic shoreline walk will take you along a blustery coastal path leading to a magnificent sight of the white chalk cliffs. The star attraction is the Seven Sisters, a section of undulating hilltops between Cuckmere Haven and Birling Gap. As well as these spectacular summits, you can also walk right down to the shoreline in places, so pack your cosie if it's a sunny day!

www.southdownsway.co.uk

PICS: ALAMY

GO BIRD SPOTTING

Walberswick Nature Reserve, Suffolk

This walk is a must for twitchers! Summer is the perfect time to spot avocets, godwits, pintails and wigeons at Walberswick. If you can tear yourself away from reed beds, estuary marshes, saline lagoons and shingle beaches, then there's a very pleasant circular walk to be had, too. From the lovely village of Southwold, you can head inland through the nature reserve and down through a small forest to the equally scenic Dunwich, before heading back along the coastal mudflats and sand dunes.

www.ifootpath.com

DUNES AND FORESTS

Holkham beach, Holkham, North Norfolk

Walk among the beautiful sand dunes that line the coast at Holkham. It's a perfect spot for a summer picnic. The beach itself is one of the largest nature reserves in the country. Begin your walk on the sandy beach and when you want to head back, dip into the pine forest that's set back from the sand for a totally different return journey. If you fancy walking a little further, Holkham Hall and grounds are about a mile from the beach car park, it's worth exploring this historic property and enjoying an ice cream in the sun at the courtyard café.   **www.holkham.co.uk**

TAKE A DIP

Dancing Ledge, South West Coast Path, Dorset

The walk along Dancing Ledge in Dorset is perfect for summer, because it allows you to see the sparkling sea below. Your walk starts in the village of Worth Matravers, where you will head west on the path for a short distance before looping around St. Aldhelm's Head and following the cliff-top path. It's on this section of the walk where you'll discover the Dancing Ledge. Centuries ago, the rocks and sea formed a circular shape made of rocks and filled with seawater gushing against the shore - it's quite a sight as the waves come crashing down. This walk wouldn't be complete without a dip, so spend some time there enjoying the water and soaking up the sun before heading back.
www.southwestcoastpath.org.uk

POLDARK WALK

Botallack mining walk, Penwith Heritage Coast, Penzance

Brood like Poldark actor Aidan Turner on the cliffs of the Cornish coast and visit the Cornish Mining World Heritage where much of the BBC drama was filmed. This walk beautifully combines historical and industrial sites with heathlands blooming with rare wild flowers. Be sure to visit the Botallack mine itself. It's situated on the tin coast that houses the iconic Crowns Engine Houses that cling to the cliffs- it's one of the most photographed engine houses in the entire World Heritage Site.
www.nationaltrust.co.uk/botallack

STARGAZING STROLL

Friar's Crag, Lake District

The open skies at Friar's Crag are a magical location for star gazing and wildlife spotting. Walk along the shore of Derwentwater on this short (0.75m) linear walk. You'll end up at Friar's Crag, a rocky cliff jutting out into the lake. Do the walk on a warm summer evening to enjoy a beautiful sunset and some spectacular views of the stars. Look up to see the Summer Triangle made up of three bright stars called Deneb, Vega and Altair as you pass the launch jetties. At Friar's Crag try to spot the Milky Way and North Star in the night sky.
www.nationaltrust.org.uk/
borrowdale-and-derwent-water

A HEATHLAND RAMBLE

Teggs Nose & Dean Valley

With a beautiful mixture of heather and harebells in bloom, this summer walk on the edge of the Peak District is perfect if you want to connect with nature. And if that's not enough to get you up the hill, then maybe the wood sage and bilberry on the moors with mountain pansies in the meadows will do the trick. Dry stone walls and sturdy barns add to the dramatic character of the steeply sided valleys while many of the hill tops are pitted with old quarries. Be sure to keep your eyes peeled for sightings of flycatchers, thrushes, treecreepers, buzzards and woodpeckers.
www.teggsnose.co.uk

Lovely lavender

Fiona Cumberpatch explains how lavender is easy to look after and with it's exotic aroma, deserves a place in any garden

Fast and easy to grow, lavender smells beautiful and keeps its soft, silvery leaves all year round. It's a garden hero, perfect for a modern plot. Grow it in pots, use it to create a fragrant hedge or add it to borders, where it will happily spill on to paths or lawn edges, flowering all summer long.

HOW TO GROW IT

Summer is when lavender looks its stunning, spiky best. But this easy-going herb is happy planted out at any time, once the soil is warm. If planting, water the roots enough to help them establish but never let your lavender sit in water. In the garden, once growing strongly, it won't need watering but plants in pots will; once a week in summer. Plant in full sun and well-drained soil.

HOW BIG DOES IT GROW?

This depends on the variety, and there are many. If you're tight for space, choose a dwarf one, such as 'Little Lottie' or 'Miss Muffet', as these will not grow taller than 30cm (1ft). For a tall plant, opt for 'Seal', with vibrant green leaves and bright purple flowers, or 'Edelweiss', which grows up to 90cm (3ft), and has bushy leave.

HOW TO KEEP IT TIDY

Prune English lavender twice a year to keep the foliage compact and stop brown woody patches.

1. When flowers have faded (late summer/early autumn), trim them and their stalks using shears for a clean snip. Cut about 2.5cm (1in) off the leafy part with secateurs, making sure that some green bits remain. The plants will look a bit like grey hedgehogs, but they'll quickly recover.

2. In late February (early March if it's been a cold winter) give a light haircut with shears. This will retain its compact, clumpy shape.

GROW A HEDGE FOR SCENT AND COLOUR

Simple and beautiful, a low lavender hedge creates a perfect feature, and it's so easy to achieve. Choose your plants carefully. For a uniform look, go for one variety, but for a softer drift of colour, opt for a few different types to vary those blue hues.

For a small, compact hedge, try 'Hidcote', which has dense, bushy grey-green foliage and dark violet flowers on upright stems. It grows to about 60cm (24in), flowers from late June onwards and won't flop over.

'Munstead' is another good choice for a smaller hedge, with its mid-green leaves and classic lavender-blue flowers. It will grow about 45cm (18in) tall and 70cm (2ft 4in) wide.

◆ Space your plants approximately 30cm (12in) apart.
◆ Dig a hole that's a bit bigger than the plant's rootball.
◆ Ease the plant out of the pot and into the soil. Replace the soil and gently firm around the base of the lavender. Water well.
◆ Water in thoroughly. After that the plant will look after itself.

DRYING LAVENDER

Dried lavender has so many uses. Put it in a simple bunch in a vase, use it to stuff sachets to add fragrance to wardrobes and ward off moths, or attach a single sprig to a gift when wrapping. Pick the flowers before they're in full bloom, when none of the small florets are fully open. The dried buds will then keep their fragrance longer, and won't fall apart as they dry out.

If you only want to harvest the lavender buds and petals for making bags, remove the stalks from the fresh lavender and keep the heads. Layer them in the bottom of a box lined with newspaper. Store in a warm, dry place such as an airing cupboard. Shake the box each day to keep the air circulating. Once the lavender is dry (after two to three weeks) rub the heads to remove the bud from the stem.

To dry in bunches, cut the lavender, leaving long stems of about 20cm (8in). Secure with an elastic band and hang upside down to dry in a warm place. Each bunch will take about two weeks to dry. You can tell when it's ready because it will feel slightly brittle and will crumble between your fingers. Remove the rubber band and arrange as you like.

Modern Gardens, hundreds of easy ideas, projects and fresh inspiration every month!

Summer fun

PIC: VISITWILTSHIRE.CO.UK

IT'S A BEAUTIFUL DAY

Amazingly, Wiltshire has three Areas of Outstanding Natural Beauty - almost half of its countryside, so you're spoilt for choice for a summer outing. The largest covers 380 square miles in the south-west of the county, Cranborne Chase and West Wiltshire Downs. Spend a day exploring charming Tisbury - the area's largest village - where you can visit the graves of Rudyard Kipling's parents in a churchyard where a 4,000-year-old yew tree grows. There's also a Grade I listed Tithe Barn (one of England's largest) open to the public for the first time ever as an arts centre, Messums Wiltshire, where there are all sorts of exhibitions and events. Visit the café while you're there, and try the barn's own blend of coffee. **Call 01747 445042 or visit http:// messumswiltshire.com**

ON YER BIKE

The Strawberry line is an ambitious project to create a 30-mile traffic-free path across Somerset from Clevedon to Shepton Mallet. At time of going to press, it was still a work in progress, but there are already completed sections for budding Bradley Wiggins to enjoy. For a relatively easy 10-mile ride, start at the Railway Inn, Yatton and pedal through to Cheddar along a former railway life. You'll pass apple orchards, wooden valleys and go through a tunnel under the Mendips, so it's a charming route for a summer's day. **For information on the Strawberry Line visit www.thestrawberryline.org.uk**

LITERARY ESCAPISM

While the summer holidays might mean the pretty town of Haworth, with its Brontë Parsonage Museum and quaint gift shops, is rather crowded, it's a great time to explore the moors made famous by the authors. Consider booking a Brontë Walks guided tour through the Worth Valley, which offers all sorts of excursions. We like the sound of picnicking in the ruins of Bolton Abbey, as well as standing on the moorlands at Ponden Kirk and imagining the romance of Heathcliff and Cathy playing out in front of you, all the while learning about the famous sisters and their novels. They also offer a Railway Children tour, featuring the historic Keighley and Worth Valley Railway - an ideal way to introduce grandchildren to a classic story.
Prices vary. Call 07749 108105 or visit www. brontewalks.co.uk

TRY SOMETHING NEW...

If Wimbledon's got you feeling inspired, it could be time to pick up a racquet yourself. It's a great way to stay in shape (an hour's game burns around 420 calories) as well as improve hand-eye coordination and make new friends.
Find local events by calling British Tennis on 020 8487 7000 or visit www.lta.org.uk/play/

◆ There's no reason to miss out if you are disabled – the Tennis Foundation encourages everyone to give the sport a go, and can help with equipment from sports wheelchairs to balls that make a noise when they bounce, to help the visually impaired.
Call 020 8487 7000 or visit www. tennisfoundation.org.uk/play-tennis/

THREE OF THE BEST...

...*picnic spots*
Pack up your bags with sandwiches and a Thermos, and enjoy the Great British countryside from the comfort of a blanket.

◆ Londoners are spoilt for choice when it comes to gorgeous green spaces, but there's something special about picnicking on Hampstead Heath, especially in the grounds of John Keats' house at the bottom of the park. Poetic feelings guaranteed.

◆ Visits to Dorset are all about good food. Pack up some clotted cream and scones and head to the dramatic Old Harry Rocks, Studland. There's an easy 3.5 mile walk where you might be lucky enough to spot peregrine falcons, and you'll get fab views over the white cliffs into the churning sea.

◆ Clamber up the edges of Britain's deepest valley for phenomenal views down to the sea. Devil's Dyke near Brighton is a lovely spot in the South Downs Way for a panoramic picnic.

COOL DOWN

If you're feeling brave and the sun is shining, why not consider a trip to one of the country's historic lidos? One of the prettiest has to be the salt water Tinside Lido in Plymouth, which was built in 1935 and boasts beautiful art deco features including a fountain. The Grade II listed building also has lovely sea views. You'll soon see why it's been voted one of the top ten outdoor pools in Europe.
Call 01752 261915 or visit www.everyoneactive. com/centre/tinside-lido

Wall-mounted

Give your home or garden a vintage vibe with these vases made from recycled preserving jars

vases

1 If you have a plain or a discoloured piece of wood, you may want to paint it before you start working with it. Use an exterior or waterproof paint and then paint the wood, leaving the first coat to dry before you add the second coat. Once the paint is dry you can begin screwing the jars on.

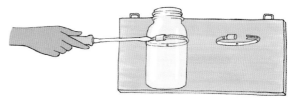

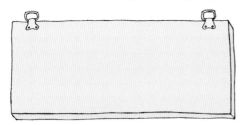

2 To attach the D-rings to the back of your piece of wood, measure in 5cm (2in) from either edge mark the points with a pencil. Place the D rings over your pencil mark with the rings over the top edge. Screw them into the wood. You may need drill holes to do this first depending on the thickness and quality of your wood.

3 Make a small mark on the central part of both of the hose clips, which should be directly opposite the clasps. With a drill make a hole where you've marked through each of the hose clips. Work out the positioning of your hose clips, making sure they're equal distance from each edge of the wood and not positioned too close together. Screw them down.

4 Slide one of the jars into a hose clip to check the fit, and then using a small screwdriver, screw the hose clip tight around the jar, to ensure the vases are securely fastened and won't fall out if the clasp is knocked suddenly (be careful not to apply too much pressure when tightening the clip because the glass may shatter.) Repeat with the second jar.

5 Once finished and the jars are securely fixed in place. Take the wood and hang the wall-mounted piece from a couple of nails or hooks screwed into the wall, wherever you want the vases on display. Add your water and your flowers to the jars. If you want to clean the jars at any point then just unscrew the hose clips and remove to clean.

YOU WILL NEED

40x20cm (16x8in) piece of wood, such as an old bit of floorboard
Waterproof paint and paintbrush
Ruler
Pencil
2 D-ring picture hangers (from hardware shops)
Small screws
Screwdriver
2 hose clips, 80-100mm (3-4in) in diameter (from hardware shops)
Drill with a metal bit
2x9cm (3in) diameter Kilner preserving jars
Small nails or hooks, for hanging the vases

Taken from: Crafting with Mason Jars and other Glass Containers by Hester van Overbeek, published by CICO Books (£12.99)

Enjoy nature

WALKING ON FALLEN LEAVES

Batsford Arboretum, Moreton-in-Marsh, Gloucestershire

Take a wander around Batsford's 56-acre arboretum, home to Britain's largest private collection of trees and shrubs. Famous for its Far Eastern species, it also houses rare species that have died out in the wild and 'Champion Trees' (exceptional examples of their species because of their size, age, rarity or historical significance). This is by far the best time of year to visit, as Batsford's colour palette goes off the scale in autumn with the flame reds, crimsons, salmon pinks and sunshine yellows of its maples and cherries.

www.batsarb.co.uk

SPOTTING RED SQUIRRELS

Allan Bank, Grasmere, Lake District

Red squirrels are in danger of extinction in England, and Grasmere is one of the few remaining places in the country where they still thrive. Take a leisurely stroll around this picturesque lakeside town, where you can see William Wordsworth's grave, Sarah Nelson's Gingerbread shop and Grasmere's beautiful crystal clear lake. Stop for a bite to eat in one of the many delightful tearooms then head to Allan Bank- the former home of Wordsworth.

Allan Bank is also a great place to see our native red squirrels. You're highly likely to spot one as the National Trust spend over £900 on feed every year! Take a stroll along the garden path to see if you can catch sight of one along the way.

www.nationaltrust.org.uk/allan-bank-and-grasmere

ANCIENT TREE WALK
Calke Abbey, Derbyshire

Be wowed by the majesty of ancient trees at Calke Abbey. Take a stroll down the Ticknall lime avenue, where you'll be flanked either side by large imposing trees that were planted to celebrate the birth of the last baronet, Sir Vauncey Harpur Crewe, in 1846. Ancient trees can be seen all over the parkland. It holds two oak trees that are 1,000 years old and a lime tree that's slowly making its way across the landscape as the branches make contact with the ground.

www.nationaltrust.org.uk/calke-abbey

PIC: NATIONAL TRUST

PICTURE PERFECT

Hardcastle Crags, West Yorkshire

Lying just west of Halifax, the valleys of Hardcastle Crags offer more than 400 acres of peaceful countryside to explore, with scenic views of deep ravines and tumbling streams.

Anyone with a craving for open spaces can take the rocky paths to the hilltops and enjoy sweeping views over the West Yorkshire landscape, while down in the woodland the oak, beech and pine trees provide vibrant bursts of autumn colour. Stepping stones and picturesque footbridges arching over the river provide a great focal point for that perfect autumn photograph.
www.nationaltrust.org.uk/hardcastle-crags

IN THE FOOTSTEPS OF POETS

Heddon Valley, North Devon - Heddon Valley to Woody Bay walk

Nestled on the West Exmoor coast it's easy to see why the Heddon Valley was a favourite with the Romantic poets. In autumn the path along the Heddon Valley to Woody Bay is full of vibrant yellow gorse, which scents the air with the smell of coconuts all the way down to the sea at Heddon's Mouth. There are also plenty of walking routes higher up, including an historic 19th century carriageway and part of the South West Coast Path, which run across some of England's most dramatic coastal cliffs. Those braving the terrain will be rewarded with stunning coastal views across the Bristol Channel to Wales.
www.nationaltrust.org.
uk/heddon-valley

AUTUMN COLOUR WALK

Belton House, Grantham, Lincolnshire

Autumn reds, yellows and golden browns can be found all over Belton, from the adventure playground and parkland, to the tranquil views overlooking the boating lakes. The magical misty mornings and crisp, clear days of autumn are an ideal time to enjoy this season's changing colours. As you explore the estate on this walk you can rustle your way through fallen leaves and enjoy the gorgeous golds and yellows of the lime trees along the cobbled drive. Closer to the house, rich ruby and russet creepers clad the honey-coloured walls of the West Courtyard, and the sweet aroma of ripening quinces fills the air.
www.nationaltrust.org.uk/belton-house

PIC: NATIONAL TRUST

SEAL SPOTTING

Marloes Peninsula, Pembrokeshire, Wales

Breathe in the spectacular view at the very tip of the Marloes Peninsula. There's a very leisurely one mile walk that features dramatic coastal scenery, with fantastic views of Pembrokeshire's islands. The walk starts at Martin's Haven car park, and follows the coastline path all the way round. In autumn you'll see purple heather and yellow gorse bushes and if you're lucky you may see seal pups. In autumn most female grey seals haul themselves ashore to give birth so this really is the best time of year to spot a pup!
www.nationaltrust.org.uk/marloes-sands

All about Acers

Lucy Bellamy explains how acers, with their compact, jewel-coloured leaves, are great in modern spaces

Acers, also known as Japanese maples, are the perfect tree for a contemporary plot. Their delicate shape and canopy of intricate, lacy leaves means they don't cast too much shade...rather a dappled light. They're even happy planted in a big pot. As the weather turns colder, acer leaves show the most amazing hues. Their foliage becomes yellow, saffron, plum, cherry and fire-engine red. They're just the job for planting in a key spot to enjoy every month of the year. As they only have shallow roots, they're safe to plant close to the house, so are ideal if you have a smaller garden.

Despite being from the same family as maple trees, acers are much smaller. Best planted in autumn, while the soil is still warm but without the challenge of settling in a new spot during heat and water shortage, these are slow-growing plants. They don't need pruning to keep them in check. A young purple-leafed tree will grow to around 1m (3ft) high and wide in five years.

Many acers available to buy are grown from seed and there are hundreds of different varieties. Acers are divided into two groups. Acer atropurpureum have red or purple leaves and acer dissectum are usually green and have finely cut (dissected) leaves. Read the plant label or check the description carefully if shopping online.

Acer atropurpureum is well-suited to pots because of its neat size and shape. It has small, deep purple leaves that are fine and feathery and shaped like the palms of hands.

Its branches are red and spread outwards so the leaves are held in layers that let the sun stream through, creating a pretty, flickering light. It turns brilliant red in autumn. Popular 'Bloodgood' has deepest purple leaves. It grows to 5m (16ft) in 20 years.

The cut-leaved maple, Acer palmatum 'Dissectum', creates a rounded dome of lacy foliage in fresh green. It grows to 2m (6ft 6in) and is a good choice for pots because of its striking, rounded structural shape.

POTTING YOUR TREE

Acers grow happily in a pot so they're great for the corner of a deck or patio, or next to the front door. They are deciduous, dropping their leaves in winter, but their patterned trunks and colourful branches create strongly decorative shapes.

1 Choose a pot at least twice the size of the container your tree is growing in. Make sure it has drainage holes in the base so it doesn't get waterlogged. Use a pebble or crock, such as a fragment of broken terracotta plant pot, to loosely cover the drainage hole and keep the compost inside the container.

2 Half fill the pot with mature plant compost, such as John Innes No. 3 (£3.67 for 20 litres, www.diy. com). It is rich in the nutrients that the tree will need.

3 Water your acer in its current container and then remove the pot. If it's tricky to do so, use a knife to cut it off rather than tugging at the trunk.

4 Stand the rootball in the middle of the new pot and check its height. The top of its soil should be 2-3cm below the rim of the pot to leave room for watering.

5 Backfill around the rootball with more compost and give it a good soak using a full watering can. The water will run out from the hole in the pot's base when the compost is soaked to the bottom.

6 Add a layer of pebbles to the top of the compost as a 'mulch'. They will help to hold moisture in the compost as well as looking decorative. Acers are shallow-rooted and prone to drying out if their soil gets too dry.

THREE OF THE BEST FOR INTENSE COLOUR

Acer palmatum 'Dissectum'
A cut-leaved maple with pretty, lacy green foliage.

Acer capillipes
A snake-bark maple with white-striped, branches and green leaves.

Acer palmatum 'Osakazuki'
A Japanese maple with green leaves edged with red.

Modern Gardens, hundreds of easy ideas, projects and fresh inspiration every month!

Colourful fun

Did you know? Leaves change colour as their green chlorophyll declines, allowing flavonoids, carotenoids and anthocyanins to show through, making them shades of red and orange. Some of these are the same chemicals that give egg yolks and carrots their colour.

WOODLAND WANDER

Enjoy the season's finery from one of the best places – indoors with a mug of tea! Look out over Grasmere's valley from Allan Bank, a National Trust property that was once home to its founder, Canon Rawnsley. Enjoy a snack in the kitchen, explore the Victorian viewing tunnel, help yourself to tea and look out of the window for red squirrels. Fido won't have to miss out either, as well-behaved pooches are welcome indoors too. Potter into the village of Grasmere, follow a woodland trail or eat a picnic in the grounds if the weather is tempting. **Tickets cost £6.80 adults, £3.40 children. Call 01539 435143 or visit www.nationaltrust.org.uk/allan-bank-and-grasmere**

SPECTACULAR SHOW

Perthshire is packed with woodlands (200,000 acres, to be precise) and Faskally Woods, on the banks of Loch Dunmore, are arguably the most fun, thanks to its creative light shows. Held annually in September/October, multi-award winning spectacular The Enchanted Forest combines music and lights, so you can experience the woodlands like never before. It's also worth a daytime visit thanks to its wide variety of tree species, which include colourful birch, aspen, oak and poplar amongst the evergreen conifers. **Dates and prices tbc. Call 0871 288 7655 or visit www.enchantedforest.org.uk**

GOTHIC HOLIDAY

When the weather's unpredictable it pays to pick a weekend break somewhere that has plenty to do outdoors and inside in the warm. Whitby is the perfect compromise. If the climate is kind, you can wander the sandy Blue Flag beaches and take photos of the elegant port, made famous as the setting for Bram Stoker's Dracula (best pack your garlic just in case!) It's not just fiction that the town is famed for – look out for the Whalebone Arch and a bronze statue which both commemorate Captain James Cook, who learnt all about sailing in Whitby. On rainy days, check the programme at the Whitby Pavilion, which offers everything from concerts to tea dances, or browse the numerous local jewellery shops for gorgeous souvenirs made of jet collected in Whitby. Whatever the weather, don't leave without a steaming fish supper from the Magpie Café, which has been serving fish and chips on the quayside for more than 75 years. It offers 20 varieties of fresh fish, and is always popular – expect to queue.

Whitby Pavilion call 01947 458899 or visit www. whitbypavilion.co.uk
Magpie Café call 01947 602058 or visit www. magpiecafe.co.uk

TRY SOMETHING NEW...

As animals fill their bellies before a long winter, autumn is the perfect time to dabble in wildlife photography. There are lots of tips and tricks, but the most commonly used one is the 'rule of thirds'. This involves imagining your frame divided into nine equal sections (three by three boxes). Positioning your subject along one of these lines – rather than slap-bang in the centre – will make it more appealing to the human eye, and make your photos stand out.

For more inspiration and ideas, visit www.yours. co.uk/wildlifephotography

THREE OF THE BEST...

...days out for autumn colour

Appreciate nature at its best with a visit to these red, orange and gold-tinged beauty spots

◆ Take your merriest men for a day out in Sherwood Forest, Nottinghamshire. There are 900 ancient oaks (one of the largest collections in western Europe) and you can even see the 800-year-old Major Oak where Robin Hood is said to have hidden.

◆ Wander 80 acres of landscaped gardens at the National Trust's Bodnant Garden, Conwy. Here you'll see hundreds of native and exotic trees, bursting with berries, fruits and russet leaves. Follow a tree trail or join a guided walk.

◆ Lace up your walking boots for a seriously picturesque 2.8 mile looped walk in Symonds Yat, in the Forest of Dean. As well as views over the River Wye and its golden forests, you'll enjoy a trip on a hand ferry.

Call ahead to check that the hand ferry is operating on 01600 890435. Download a route at www.forestry.gov.uk

WILD TIMES

If you've ever wanted to watch the drama of deer rutting season unfold, now is the time. Galloway Forest Park is an ideal spot, as there are resident red deer stags who will be battling it out for the local ladies. If you're not lucky enough to spot any, follow the Galloway Red Kite Trail along Loch Ken instead and keep your eyes peeled for birds of prey. Then visit Bellymach Hill Farm near Laurieston, where farmer Ann Johnstone feeds the kites each day at 2pm.

Pretty Pinks

*Summer flowers may have gone from the garden,
but you can still have beautiful blooms indoors*

YOU WILL NEED

Size 2 white coffee filters (available in supermarkets)
Scissors and scissors with zigzag blades (pinking shears)
4.5cm (1in) wide white crêpe paper streamer
White (PVA) glue
Pink tissue paper

Water-soluble pink felt-tip pen
Water and paintbrush
Masking tape
Wire for stem, pre-covered with paper
White crêpe paper
Spray adhesive
Green watercolour paint

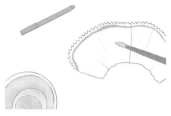

7 Cut the covered wire to the stem length you want and paint it green with a little watercolour. Make three slight angles along the stem for a natural look. Trim the flower base to 2.5cm (1in) and push the stem firmly up into the flower.

1 Each flower uses three filters. Tear off the side and bottom seam of each, fold twice into a smaller segment and cut a zigzag edge along the top. Trim off the bottom into a semicircle.

4 On the third filter, trim a curve at the top corners using zigzag scissors, then draw a 3mm (1/8in) thick line 6mm (in) down from the top edge with a felt-tip pen. Brush a line of clean water just underneath this line so the colour bleeds nicely. Add more water if necessary so the colour bleeds to the top edge. Let it dry.

8 Cut two pieces of white crêpe paper. Stick together with spray adhesive. Paint both sides with the watercolour. Cut a piece of crêpe paper 2x3in. (5x7.5cm) and paint it. Cut out a double leaf and snip irregular triangles top and bottom.

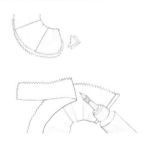

2 Cut a 43cm (17in) length of crêpe streamer, fold it over and over to make a small rectangle and cut a zigzag along the top edge. Open and glue it around the inside top edge of the first filter so it sticks out 3mm (1/2in). Pleat the bottom of the streamer as you go so it fits the curve. Trim curves at the two top corners with zigzag scissors.

5 Make another crêpe paper edge on the inside top edge of the third filter in the same way as in Step 2, but this time position it slightly below the filter edge.

9 Cover the masking tape under the flower head with glue and mould the base shape around it.

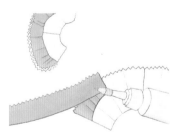

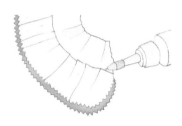

3 Cut a long strip of pink tissue paper 4.5cm (1in) deep. Cut a zigzag along one long side and use it to make an edging on the inside top edge of the second filter, as in Step 2. Add a second edging on the outside top edge with another length of crêpe streamer, as in Step 2.

6 To make the flower centre, roll the first filter up with the crêpe paper outside, pleating the bottom edge from time to time as you roll. Hold the shape firmly at the bottom. Add the second filter next, with the pink tissue on the inside. Add the third filter last, with the crêpe paper on the outside.

10 Pierce a large enough hole in the centre of the double leaf for the stem to fit through. Place a dab of glue on the stem at the top and push the leaf into it. Pinch the leaf around the stem.

Taken from Paper Flowers, published by CICO Books, rrp £12.99

Wrap up warm

A WALK IN THE PARK

Blenheim Great Park, Oxfordshire

Blenheim Palace under snow with its frozen lake and the screams of children on toboggans is an experience not to be missed, but it's just as delightful without snow!

Most visitors stay in the vicinity of the palace itself but there's so much more to see – including the Column of Victory to the north and the delightful High Park woods area to the south west.

The park, designed by Capability Brown, is now home to several Sites of Special Interest including the Great Lake and ancient oaks in High Park.
www.blenheimpalace.com

MISTY RIVER RAMBLE

Tintern Abbey and Devil's Pulpit, Wye Valley, Monmouthshire

Tintern's 12th century Cistercian abbey fell into romantic ruin after the Dissolution of the Monasteries and has been mythologised by poets and painters (most famously Wordsworth and Turner) ever since. On a crisp winter's morning, with frost on the ground and mist over the River Wye, it's a beautiful place to explore. You can do a three-and-a-half-mile walk that will reward you with a view of the abbey and river from the Devil's Pulpit.
www.visitwales.com/explore/south-wales/wye-valley-vale-usk/tintern-abbey

WINTER WILDLIFE WALK

Holy Island, Lindisfarne, Northumberland

This walk is a thrilling mix of stirring seascapes, religious mysticism, Anglo Saxon history and the ghosts of marauding Vikings on Northumberland's wild and stormy coast. You'll be walking in the footsteps of the saints and early Christian pilgrims, with Lindisfarne Castle, a garden designed by Gertrude Jekyll and the ruined priory the centrepiece of the route.

The winter wildlife on Lindisfarne's National Nature Reserve is guaranteed to provide some good sightings, with thousands of migrating birds and, if you're lucky, grey seals, porpoises and dolphins.
www.lindisfarne.org.uk

Winter walks

WALK WITH DINOSAURS

Dinosaur coastal trail, Isle of Wight

The Isle of Wight is the undisputed dinosaur capital of Great Britain and features in the top 6 'best locations' in the world for dinosaur remains. There are 6 meteorite locations dotted along the dinosaur coastal trail between Yaverland (nr. Sandown) and The Needles. Winter is a great time to do this walk as you 'll stand a greater chance of seeing the dinosaur fossil footprints when the tide is out. The Dinosaur Isle museum in Sandown organises guided fossil walks in Yaverland, Shanklin and Brook Bay throughout the year. They last up to two hours and are suitable for all ages.
www.redfunnel.co.uk

BRONTË MOORLAND WALK

Brontë Walk, Haworth, Yorkshire

Charlotte Brontë's spirit lives on, with those of her sisters and brother, on Haworth Moors, which are at their wildest and most atmospheric in winter. This walk takes you out of Haworth, the village where the Brontë sisters lived and wrote, along pathways they walked and through the moorland

that inspired them. Beginning near the church that holds the family vault, you'll walk up to the Brontë waterfalls, described by Charlotte Brontë as 'fine indeed', then up again to Top Withens, the supposed setting of Wuthering Heights. Remember that 'wuthering' is a Yorkshire word for stormy weather, so be sure to take a waterproof!
www.haworth-village.org.uk

STEP INTO A PAINTING

Constable Walk, Dedham Vale, Essex

Explore the picturesque Stour Valley and Dedham Vale made famous by the 18th century paintings of John Constable. You're probably used to seeing Constable's landscapes on biscuit tins and calendars, but seeing them in person, especially when they're stripped bare in winter and empty of other walkers, can bring about a new-found appreciation. This three-mile walk along the banks of the River Stour will take you to Fen Bridge, the 'dry dock', Bridge Cottage, Flatford Mill and Willy Lott's Cottage (Hay Wain) and long views over the surrounding water meadows.
www.nationaltrust.org.uk/flatford

WILD CATTLE AND PONY WALK

Wicken Fen, Ely, Cambridgeshire

From gentle strolls on the all-weather boardwalk around Sedge Fen, to longer walks exploring new wetland habitats, there are plenty of opportunities to spot amazing wildlife at this nature reserve. This National Trust property is a haven for birds, plants, insects and mammals. Keep a look out for hen and marsh harriers, short-eared owls and Wicken's herds of Highland cattle and Konik ponies. After a stroll you can warm up in the William Thorpe visitor centre and reward yourself with a hot drink and slice of cake at the tea room.
www.wicken.org.uk

PICS: NLAMY

Heavenly Hellebores

In rose pinks, slate greys and pretty speckled whites, Lucy Bellamy shows that hellebores are perfect for pots and tricky spots

One flower that likes a challenge is the hellebore. It blooms in winter, amid the frost, snow and rain, and in the loveliest of colours. Despite its pretty nature it's a robust little flower that's happy in a tricky spot. Plant a hellebore - especially a pale one - in a shady corner and it'll shine brightly, and more importantly, it will thrive. At the base of a tree or shrub where most plants will struggle to settle, the delicate, nodding blooms of a hellebore will create a fantastic layer of colour. These are early-flowering plants that mix easily with other blooms, braving the snow and wet. They also continue to flower for weeks and weeks, and so make perfect candidates for brilliant seasonal pots. The best time to buy a hellebore is when they are in flower as there are lots of different ones to choose from. Buying them in bloom allows you to see the flowers and choose a favourite. They vary

enormously, growing in a huge array of colours. Think pinks, reds and damsons, freckled whites and creams, slate greys and almost blacks. Some flowers have simple open shapes, others are fancier with contrast-colour edging or more than one row of petals.

The best place to grow a hellebore in your garden is an empty patch of soil where other plants will struggle. Choose somewhere that's not too far from the house so you'll be tempted to venture into the cold to enjoy the flowers. Planting is as simple as digging a hole as wide and as deep as the plant's roots in their pot, and popping it in the ground, keeping the top of its compost level with the garden soil and giving it a splash of water with a watering can. It's also a good idea to add a spadeful of multi-purpose compost to the hole, as it will give your new arrival an extra boost.

FOUR WAYS WITH HELLEBORES IN POTS

◆ Hellebores are brilliant in seasonal pots. They flower for ages with lots of blooms and don't grow too big. Once planted, the flowers will come back every year. For an early-flowering combination team Hellebore 'Anna's Red', evergreen fern and snakeshead fritillary for a stylish green and plum combination, perfect for a shady spot. Try it by the back door in a north-facing garden or in a porch, where the pot will have some protection from the weather. Water it just enough to keep the compost damp.

◆ Go mad with a variety of shapes and colours. Try Hellebore argutifolius, Viola 'Orange Sorbet', Hyacinth 'Delft Blue', Anemone blanda and variegated ivy. The holly-leafed hellebore, H argutifolius, works as a green foil for the zingy brights. Pinch the flowers off the viola as they fade to keep it blooming for longer, and snip back the ivy if it straggles. You can expect clouds of fragrance from the hyacinths, too.

◆ The simple white flowers of Hellebore niger shine against green foliage. Pair with colourful winter stems, like those of golden twig dogwood, which add height and shape. Their colour picks up the bright yellow of centres of the hellebore flowers.

◆ Hellebore niger, winter heather and snowdrops offer a one plant, one pot approach, which works because the pots and the flowers all share pretty pale tones.

PERFECT POTTING PRACTICE

◆ Choose a pot that's big enough to comfortably accommodate the roots of the plants you want to grow. Before you buy, stand the plants in the pot while still in their plastic containers, to check the size. Make sure the pot is deep enough to fit them in with the top of their compost level with the top of the pot, and that there's some space around them for their roots to spread.

◆ Use multi-purpose compost to half fill the pot. Tap the plants out of their pots and gently tease out some of the roots with your fingers. Position them inside, arranging them until you're happy.

◆ Fill in the gaps around them with more compost, and water in using a full can.

Modern Gardens, hundreds of easy ideas, projects and fresh inspiration every month!

Whatever the weather

CAKE TIME

Whether you love to go up hill and down dale, or would frankly be happier experiencing the winter weather through a window, Bakewell in Derbyshire has something for everyone. Keen outdoor types can wander the picturesque Peak District to their hearts' content, while those who prefer a steaming pot of tea and some homemade snacks will find plenty of tempting tearooms and cosy pubs. Naturally the Bakewell pudding is the teatime snack to sink your teeth into, and arguably the best can be found at the Old Original Bakewell Pudding Shop. Foodies will also enjoy the town's market, which runs every Monday. If your break is pre-Christmas, pop into the elegant Chatsworth House (which many believe was the inspiration for Mr Darcy's estate in Pride and Prejudice) to see its beautiful festive displays.

Old Original Bakewell Pudding Shop call 01629 812193 or visit www.bakewellpuddingshop. co.uk

Chatsworth Estate house and garden tickets £21.90 adults, £14 children. Call 01246 565 300 or visit www.chatsworth.org

KEEPING COSY

For a snug pub, with a view of (hopefully) snow-dusted hills, spend a weekend - or more - in the pretty Scottish town of Melrose. It's an extremely pretty area, nestled beside the Eildon hills, and has a special spot in the hearts of sports fans as the birthplace of Rugby Sevens. It's now easier than ever to reach, thanks to the Borders Railway which opened in 2015 along the old Waverley Line (decommissioned in 1969) and offers a rather scenic route from Edinburgh that takes just over an hour. There are plenty of pubs where you can enjoy a wee dram, as well as plenty of restaurants serving Borders lamb and local smoked salmon, fresh from the river Tweed. Burn off the excess with a frosty river walk, or if you're feeling adventurous, a hike in the Eildon Hills. Pay a visit to the ruined Melrose Abbey where there's a buried casket believed to contain the heart of Robert the Bruce.

Melrose Abbey, tickets £5.50 adults, £3.30 children, under 5s free. Call 01896 822562 or visit www.historicenvironment.scot

> **Did you know?**
> The valley of Garbh Choire Mor, in the Cairngorms, has been named the snowiest place in Britain. Several places in the Cairngorms experience snow on average for 76 days per year.

CHRISTMAS WELLS ARE RINGING

Plan a visit to England's smallest city for a pre-Christmas break. Wells, in Somerset, is packed with festive charm - think tasteful fairy lights and a big Christmas tree. There are always plenty of seasonal activities to try at Bishop's Palace and Gardens too, so make sure to check before you go and book in advance. Do your shopping in the lovely boutiques and independent shops that line the Medieval streets, and if you're lucky your trip might coincide with the city's Christmas market (date tbc). Meanwhile, a visit to the stunning cathedral (parts of which date back to 1175) is sure to give you festive tingles, particularly if you manage to catch a carol concert there.

Bishop's Palace and Gardens tickets £7.99 adults, £3.35 children, under 5s free. Call 01749 988111 or visit https://bishopspalace.org.uk

Find information on cathedral carol concerts at www.wellscathedral.org.uk/ or book tickets on 01749 672773

TRY SOMETHING NEW...

For a winter sport without the hair-raise-factor of skiing, why not consider curling? Played on ice, this workout is relatively gentle but will improve your muscle strength and fitness, as well as being a great way to make friends. England has a centre in Kent; Wales has a centre in Queensferry; while Scotland has numerous centres!

Find details on the centres at www.trycurling.com

THREE OF THE BEST...

...blustery beaches

There's something special about British beaches off-season. There may not be ice cream vans or frolicking children - or sunshine for that matter - but kicking up the sand on a winter's day is one of life's great pleasures.

◆ Walberswick, Suffolk. A busy spot over the summer, a winter visit is a nice opportunity to enjoy the Area of Outstanding Natural Beauty without the crowds. Bird watchers will be in their element thanks to the rich heath and marshland which attracts all sorts, including marsh and hen harriers, peregrines, merlin and rough-legged buzzards.

◆ Horsey, Norfolk. Wildlife enthusiasts have no doubt already visited the resident seals who loll on the Norfolk shorelines, but did you also know that it's worth training your binoculars towards the sea over the winter? Humpback whales have been seen before, so keep your eyes peeled!

◆ Robin Hoods Bay, Yorkshire. The perfect place for a bit of fossil hunting, and winter means you might just have the cliff-fringed beach to yourself. There are lots of nice pubs nearby to warm yourself up in after a seaside stroll too.

Snuggle up!

Snuggle up and keep warm with this ribbon and lace-trimmed hot water bottle cover

YOU WILL NEED

Calico 46x30.5cm (18x12in)
Fabric for the back section
46x30.5cm (18x12in)
Fabric for lining 46x61cm (18x24in)
Wadding 46x61cm (18x24in)
Bias binding 107cm (42in)
15 strips of fabric, lace and ribbon,
various widths, 28cm (11in) long
Ribbon for ties 81cm (32in)
Card and pen for template
Scissors
Dressmaking pins
Sewing machine and thread

1 Draw around a hot water bottle on a piece of card, leaving a 5cm (2in) border. Cut out the template you've made, then fold in half lengthways to make sure it's symmetrical. Unfold and use to cut a hot water bottle shape from the calico, one from the fabric for the back section, and two shapes from the lining fabric.

4 From the curve of the 'shoulder' of the water bottle shape, sew round the bottom to the same point on the other shoulder, leaving the top open to slip the hot water bottle inside. Quilt each side of the seams, trimming the excess fabric. Place the two lining fabrics right sides together and sew in the same way.

2 Take one of the 15 strips of fabric and lay it right side up across the bottom of the calico. Place the second strip right side down, overlapping the first at a slight angle, and then sew together across the top. Fold over the side of the strip that isn't sewn up so it sits across the calico, creating a multi-fabric effect as seen in the picture above. Repeat until the calico is covered. Stitch lace across the seams to make it look pretty.

3 Take the cover and place it right side up on top of one piece of the wadding. Lay the back section right side down on top of this, and then finally top it off with the last piece of wadding.

Taken from Quilted Covers & Cosies, by Debbie Shore. Published by Search Press, priced £5.59. Photography by Garie Hind

5 Turn the outer bag the right way out. Push the lining, inside out, into the main cover, which should now be right side out. Cut the ribbon into four pieces, and then pin so they face inwards to the neck on both sides of your bottle cover - these are to tie it up when your hot water bottle is placed inside.

6 Pin then sew the bias binding around the opening, trapping the ribbon in the stitching. Remove the pins then add a hot water bottle!

Notable dates 2018

New Year's Day (Bank Holiday observed)	Monday January 1
Bank Holiday (Scotland)	Tuesday January 2
Epiphany	Saturday January 6
Burns' Night	Thursday January 25
Shrove Tuesday (Pancake Day)	Tuesday February 13
Ash Wednesday	Wednesday February 14
Valentine's Day	Wednesday February 14
Chinese New Year (Dog)	Friday February 16
St David's Day	Thursday March 1
Commonwealth Day	Monday March 12
St Patrick's Day (Bank Holiday N. Ireland/Eire)	Saturday March 17
Mothering Sunday	Sunday March 11
British Summer Time begins (clocks go forward)	Sunday March 25
Palm Sunday	Sunday March 25
Maundy Thursday	Thursday March 29
First Day of Passover (Jewish Holiday)	Friday March 30
Good Friday (Bank Holiday)	Friday March 30
Easter Sunday	Sunday April 1
Easter Monday (Bank Holiday)	Monday April 2
St George's Day	Monday April 23
May Day (Early May Bank Holiday)	Monday May 7
Ascension Day	Thursday May 10
First Day of Ramadan (Islam)	Tuesday May 15
Spring Bank Holiday	Monday May 28
Fathers' Day	Sunday June 17
Summer Solstice (Longest day)	Thursday June 21
Armed Forces Day	Saturday June 30
American Independence Day	Wednesday July 4
Battle of the Boyne (Holiday N. Ireland)	Thursday July 12
St Swithun's Day	Sunday July 15
Summer Bank Holiday (Scotland / Eire)	Monday August 6
Summer Bank Holiday	Monday August 27
Jewish New Year (Rosh Hashanah)	Sunday September 9
Islamic New Year	Tuesday September 11
Trafalgar Day	Sunday October 21
British Summer Time ends (clocks go back)	Sunday October 28
Hallowe'en	Wednesday October 31
All Saints' Day	Thursday November 1
Guy Fawkes' Night	Monday November 5
Diwali (Hindu Festival)	Wednesday November 7
Remembrance Sunday	Sunday November 11
St Andrew's Day	Friday November 30
First Sunday in Advent	Sunday December 2
Winter Solstice (Shortest day)	Friday December 21
CHRISTMAS DAY	Tuesday December 25
BOXING DAY	Wednesday December 26
New Year's Eve/Hogmanay	Monday December 31

DIARY 2018

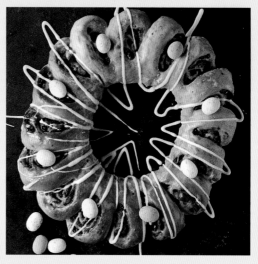

31 SUNDAY

1 MONDAY

2 TUESDAY

3 WEDNESDAY

4 THURSDAY

5 FRIDAY

6 SATURDAY

Blast from the past

DOUGHNUTS & CO

Suited and booted

In 1969 I left work on a Friday and started work at Freeman, Hardy & Willis's shoe shop on the Monday. The manager was very strict and you were addressed as either Miss or Mrs and your surname – never by your first name. He was behind the counter in the ladies department on the ground floor while I worked on the first floor in the children and men's department.

The days seemed endless, from 9am to 5.30pm (6pm on Fridays and Saturdays), but we did have two breaks as well as a long lunch break of one hour and fifteen minutes.

My mum opened my brown pay packet and gave me two pounds and ten shillings. We got a staff discount of twenty-five per cent so I had lots of shoes including a pair of wet-look stretch boots in white. On my day off, I used to go shopping in Leeds.

The customers usually paid in cash and we used to send it in a shute downstairs. I remember the first credit card I accepted. We had a machine to swipe it over a paper slip and thought the customer must be very rich to have a card.
Sylvia Foster, by email

No 1 this week

1954 Eddie Calvert: Oh, Mein Papa
Eddie Calvert with Norrie Paramor & His Orchestra started a nine-week run at the top of the UK singles chart on January 2, 1954. This instrumental version of a German folk song was the first No.1 to be recorded at Abbey Road Studios in London. At the same time Eddie Fisher's version (with lyrics) was topping the US charts.

What a good idea

Stiff jar of leftover Christmas pickle you just can't seem to open? Stick duct tape around the jar lid, leaving a piece of tape free at the end to hold on to. Pull on that loose end firmly to give you more leverage and the jar should start turning open more easily.

Bizarre Britain

On New Year's Day hardy souls hurl themselves off Mappleton Bridge, Derbyshire into the icy waters of the river 30ft beneath, before swimming and then running towards a finish line. It's a charity fundraising event that's been going on for more than 20 years. The prize? A brass iron for the ladies and a brass monkey for the gents.

Portrait of a star

DIRK BOGARDE

BORN: **March 28, 1921**
DIED: **May 8, 1999**
KNOWN FOR: **The Night Porter, Death In Venice, Doctor In The House**
HE SAID: **"I don't lose my temper often; about once every 20 years, perhaps."**

Recipe of the week

GARDENER'S PIE

Serves: 4 Preparation time: 20 mins
Cooking time: 1hr 10 mins

1kg (2lb 4oz) potatoes, peeled and cut into chunks
1 large onion, chopped
4 roughly chopped celery sticks
4 large carrots, peeled and diced
2 garlic cloves, finely chopped
4 large parsnips, peeled and diced
1 large bag of spinach
500ml (18floz) vegetable stock
150g (5oz) of peas
2 tsp mustard powder
1 tbsp finely-chopped fresh parsley

1 Preheat the oven to 220°C/425°F/Gas Mark 7. Cook the potatoes, peeled and cut into chunks, in boiling water for 12-15 mins, or until they are tender.

2 Meanwhile, over a medium heat, add the onion, celery sticks, carrots, garlic, parsnips and spinach and stir-fry for 10 mins until the vegetables are starting to colour but are still crunchy.

3 Add 300ml (½ pt) of the vegetable stock, peas and mustard powder and stir. Season to taste and spoon into a medium-size pie dish.

4 Drain the potatoes and return them to the saucepan along with the remaining stock. Mash until smooth then spoon on top of the vegetables, smooth with a fork and bake for 25-30 mins or until golden.

5 Scatter over the finely chopped fresh parsley and serve.

From Slimming World's Veggie Deluxe £4.95

7 SUNDAY

8 MONDAY

9 TUESDAY

10 WEDNESDAY

11 THURSDAY

12 FRIDAY

13 SATURDAY

Blast from the past

Humour in uniform

I am now 86 years old but still remember clearly every detail of a strange incident that happened when I was in the RAF, stationed at Weeton, just outside Blackpool.

RAF Weeton was a training camp for drivers, mechanics, blacksmiths etcetera, so there were many airmen from all over the country based there.

For reasons of security, our billets were locked in the morning and the keys handed in to the guardroom until four o'clock in the afternoon.

When we took our driving test in Blackpool we found that after the test, which took only an hour, we had nothing to do for the rest of the day so we climbed in through the window of our billet where we lay on our beds reading papers and comics.

An officer who happened to be passing by spotted us and all thirteen of us were charged with breaking and entering. As a result we were punished by 'defaulters' - in other words, confined to camp for fourteen days.

Imagine that - charged with breaking and entering for being in our own billet and lying on our own beds. Military life could be hard to fathom at times!

John Burns, Derby

No 1 this week

1971 Clive Dunn: Granddad
While starring in Dad's Army, Clive Dunn met bassist Herbie Flowers at a party and challenged him to write a song for him. Granddad was released in November 1970 and, following some promotion on children's TV shows such as Basil Brush and with DJ Tony Blackburn claiming it as his favourite record, in January 1971 it reached No.1 and stayed there for three weeks

What a good idea

If you need to return an item to a shop after Christmas or from the sales and don't have the receipt, don't panic. All you need is proof that you bought the item and when, so a bank statement, the price tag or guarantee would be worth taking to the store instead.

Bizarre Britain

For 700 years, Ponteland, Northumberland has been seeing in the New Year with a wheelbarrow race! Part of a tradition that can be traced back to the 14th century when the Lord of the Manor encouraged locals to scour the countryside for food, today residents wheel each other around the village to raise funds for charity.

Portrait of a star

DEAN MARTIN

BORN: **June 7, 1917**
DIED: **December 25, 1995**
KNOWN FOR: **Oceans 11, Robin and the Seven Hoods, The Dean Martin Show**
HE SAID: **"I'd hate to be a teetotaller. Imagine getting up in the morning and knowing that's as good as you're going to feel all day."**

Recipe of the week

CHICKEN AND BEAN SOUP

Serves: 4 Preparation time: 15 mins Cooking time: 15 mins

2 tsp olive oil
1 chopped onion
800ml (1pt 3floz) of vegetable stock
400g (14oz) chopped tomatoes
400g (14oz) can of cannellini beans, drained,
75g (3oz) orzo pasta,
150g (5oz) shredded cooked chicken
150g (5oz) whole green beans
Handful fresh parsley

1 Heat the oil in a pan and gently fry the onion until golden brown.
2 Add the stock to the pan and mix in the chopped tomatoes, beans, orzo, cooked chicken and whole green beans. Stir.
3 Bring the pan to the boil, then cover and reduce the heat down to a low simmer for 10 mins, stirring occasionally.
4 Once it's thickened up and the pasta and vegetables are all cooked, serve garnished with some fresh parsley.
www.waitrose.com

14 SUNDAY

15 MONDAY

16 TUESDAY

17 WEDNESDAY

18 THURSDAY

19 FRIDAY

20 SATURDAY

Blast from the past

Sheer delight

I remember my first pair of stockings,
Thirty denier with a seam down the back.
I thought they were really terrific,
But in fact they were wrinkly and slack,
'Cos my legs were a little bit skinny,
And the stockings were really quite cheap,
So, in spite of my desperate efforts,
I never quite managed to keep
The seams straight where they should be;
They'd each take a different route,
And my pins looked at each other
As if in a major dispute.
But my legs grew a little more shapely,
And stockings improved somewhat too.
They were finer and much more attractive,
And became seamless (which was long overdue!)
But soon mini-skirts were the fashion
And stockings met their demise.
We couldn't keep wearing suspenders
When our skirts came up to our thighs.
Then tights were the latest 'must-have'
So stockings were left far behind.
Now the only stockings that I'll ever wear,
I suppose, are the dreary surgical kind.

Delia Bennett, Leicestershire

No 1 this week

**1972 New Seekers:
I'd Like to Teach the World to Sing**
The song started as a jingle on a Coca-Cola
TV ad and originally included the line, 'I'd
like to buy the world a Coke.' The iconic ad
featured a multi-cultural group of teenagers
on top of a hill singing and was so popular
the New Seekers single (reworked to take out
references to Coke) sold 96,000 copies in one
day. The single eventually sold more than
12 million copies worldwide and Coca-Cola
donated their $80,000 royalties to UNICEF.

What a good idea

Save yourself the cost of a supermarket kitchen spray by making your own. Simply fill a large jar with orange peel and top up with white vinegar. Leave this to steep for a fortnight and then strain into an old spray bottle. The spray will be perfect for cutting through grease as well as getting rid of ants.

Bizarre Britain

For centuries, the South West of England has been wassailing to mark old Twelfth Night. Wassailing is a traditional ceremony where merrymakers go from house to house singing, banging pots and pans and spreading good wishes. In some cider-producing areas trees are blessed with a piece of toast soaked in warm ale, in the hope of a good harvest ahead.

Portrait of a star

GRACE KELLY

BORN: **November 12, 1929**
DIED: **September 14, 1982**
KNOWN FOR: **Rear Window, To Catch A Thief, High Society**
SHE SAID: **"My father had a very simple view of life: you don't get anything for nothing. Everything has to be earned, through work, persistence and honesty."**

Recipe of the week

EVE'S PUDDING

Serves: 6 Preparation time: 20 mins
Cooking time: 35 mins

700g (1½ lb) Bramley cooking apples, peeled cored and cut into 2-3cm chunks
250g (9oz) fresh blackberries
100g (4oz) caster sugar
½ tsp ground cinnamon
2 tbsp fresh lemon juice
Finely grated zest of 1 lemon
2 large eggs
½ tsp vanilla extract
75g (3oz) plain flour

1 Preheat the oven to 200°C/180°C/Gas Mark 6. Put the apples, all but eight blackberries, 50g (2oz) of the sugar, the cinnamon, lemon juice and zest in a saucepan.
2 Cover and cook over a medium heat for 6-8 mins, or until the fruit is soft but still holding its shape. Spoon everything into an ovenproof dish and leave to cool.
3 Put the eggs, the remaining sugar and vanilla extract in a heatproof bowl and place over a pan of gently simmering water. Whisk until the mixture is pale, creamy and thick.
4 Remove the bowl from the heat and sift over half the flour and fold it in. Sift the remaining flour and fold it in.
5 Pour the mixture over the fruit and dot the reserved blackberries on top. Bake for 25 mins, or until the sponge is well risen, golden and firm. Sprinkle with a little icing sugar.

Comfort Food – Without the Calories by Justine Pattison, published by Orion Books

21 SUNDAY

22 MONDAY

23 TUESDAY

24 WEDNESDAY

25 THURSDAY

26 FRIDAY

27 SATURDAY

Blast from the past

Chips with everything

In the 1960s when I was in my teens my parents owned a chip shop in Lancashire. My mother, who was an excellent baker, used to make her own steak puddings and large Cornish pasties. The mushy peas were made from dried peas steeped in water with a colouring agent.

As well as running the chip shop they looked after my younger cousin who was about three years old and loved to stand on a chair at the sink washing the baking tins.

In the evenings I used to sit in the shop refilling the salt and vinegar pots and tearing up the newspapers that were used to wrap the fish and chips. It was also my job to pass over the bottles of pop (Vimto and Sarsaparilla).

There was a cellar under the shop where the potatoes were washed, then 'eyed' (having the black spots removed) before being placed in a separate hand-operated machine to make them into chips. I didn't mind using the chip machine but I hated seeing the raw fish being cut up. I didn't even like the taste of cooked fish!

The photo shows my friends and cousins outside the chip shop.
Janet Dandy, Burnley

No 1 this week

1958 Elvis Presley: Jailhouse Rock
Originally released in the US in September 1957 to coincide with the release of the film of the same name Jailhouse Rock wasn't released in the UK until January the following year. It was the first record ever to go straight into the UK charts at No.1, where it stayed for three weeks. The B-side was Treat Me Nice – another song from the film's soundtrack.

What a good idea

Broken nail? Grab a tea bag. Cut open the bag and empty out the tea, then cut a piece of the tea bag mesh big enough to cover the split in your nail. Paint your nail with base coat and while wet, place over the tea bag square. Leave to dry and add another base coat, then a coloured layer.

Bizarre Britain

The January tradition of Haxey Hood in Lincolnshire recreates the story of Lady de Mowbray who in the 14th Century donated 13 acres of land to Haxey after a local labourer found her lost silk riding hood. Today, villagers sing through the streets and tackle each other to get hold of a Sway Hood thrown into the crowd.

Portrait of a star

HUMPHREY BOGART

BORN: **December 25, 1899**
DIED: **January 14, 1957**
KNOWN FOR: **Casablanca, The Maltese Falcon, The African Queen**
HE SAID: **"I was born when you kissed me. I died when you left me. I lived a few weeks while you loved me."**

Recipe of the week

MACARONI CHEESE

Serves: 2 Preparation time: 15 mins
Cooking time: 45-50 mins

300g (11oz) macaroni
25g (1oz) flour
25g (1oz) low-fat margarine
600ml (1 pt) skimmed milk
150g (5oz) reduced-fat cheddar
Salt and pepper to taste
75g (3oz) broccoli florets
75g (3oz) cauliflower florets
40g (1½ oz) wholemeal breadcrumbs
1 pinch cayenne pepper

1 Preheat oven to 170°C/325°F/Gas Mark 4. Boil the cauliflower and broccoli florets for 7 mins.

2 In a saucepan melt the margarine, remove from the heat and stir in the flour. Return to the heat and gradually add the milk to make a smooth sauce.

3 Grate the cheese and add. Heat until the cheese has melted and the sauce is thick. Season to taste.

4 Cook the macaroni for 10-12 mins. When the macaroni is cooked, stir into the sauce along with the cauliflower and broccoli florets.

5 Put the mixture in a baking dish. Mix the breadcrumbs and the cayenne pepper and sprinkle on top. Cook for 35-40 mins or until golden brown.
www.alpro.com

28 SUNDAY

29 MONDAY

30 TUESDAY

31 WEDNESDAY

1 THURSDAY

2 FRIDAY

3 SATURDAY

Blast from the past

Fairytale of New York

In 1987, when I was 18, I was working in New York as an au pair and my friend Lynda was also an au pair in Connecticut. We used to meet at Grand Central station and go shopping before going to a restaurant or to a club. At that time, we English girls were much admired and spoiled. Everyone wanted to hear about Liverpool and the Beatles.

One night we were in Jilly's, a club made famous by Frank Sinatra, when Christopher Connelly walked in with a group of friends. At that time he was the star of the American soap, Peyton Place. We asked for his autograph and he chatted to us. Later, I noticed he was looking over at me and smiling. When his group got up to leave, one of them came over to say Chris would like us to join him at another club.

We went, of course, and that was the start of a lovely, short romance between Chris and myself. That night he took me home in his chauffered car. We had romantic times together before he had to return to California. We wrote for a while and I kept his letters for many years.
Kathie Marshall, Pewsey

No 1 this week

1971 George Harrison: My Sweet Lord
George Harrison's solo record, My Sweet Lord topped charts worldwide and was the biggest-selling single of 1971 in the UK and the first No.1 by an ex-Beatle. Later the song was at the centre of a copyright infringement case that had repercussions throughout the music industry. The courts found in favour of the complaint that Harrison was found to have subconsciously plagiarised He's So Fine, a 1963 hit for the New York girl group the Chiffons.

What a good idea

Give your jewellery a new lease of life with the help of some handy tin foil. Line a bowl with foil, fill it with hot water and a tablespoon of bleach-free washing powder. Drop in your jewellery and soak it for a minute then rinse and air dry. This method works well for your silverware, too.

Bizarre Britain

Send in the clowns to Dalston, east London! Since 1946, the Holy Trinity Church there has welcomed a congregation of clowns for the annual clowns' church service held on the first Sunday in February. The service takes place in memory of Joseph Grimaldi, the entertainer who invented the classic clown.

Portrait of a star

CHARLTON HESTON

BORN: **October 4, 1923**
DIED: **April 5, 2008**
KNOWN FOR: **Ben-Hur, Planet of the Apes, Touch of Evil**
HE SAID: **"I have played three presidents, three saints and two geniuses. If that doesn't create an ego problem, nothing does."**

Recipe of the week

COCONUT AND PRAWN SOUP

Serves: 2 Preparation time: 5 mins Cooking time: 10 mins

100g (3½ oz) rice noodles
1 tbsp oil
1 tbsp laksa/curry paste
180g raw prawns
100g (3½oz) asparagus spears
500ml (18floz) boiling water
250ml (9floz) coconut milk
2 eggs, hard-boiled, peeled and halved
15g (½oz) macadamia nuts, toasted and roughly chopped
1 lime cut into wedges
1 handful fresh coriander
1 handful fresh basil

1 Place the noodles in a bowl and pour over enough hot water to cover them, put to one side and allow to soften.
2 Heat the oil in a wok, add the laksa/curry paste and cook for 2-3 mins.
3 Add the prawns, asparagus, hot water and coconut milk.
4 Simmer gently for 5 mins, until the prawns are pink and cooked through. Drain the noodles and divide between two bowls, ladle in the hot laksa/curry paste and top with the hard-boiled eggs and toasted nuts.
5 Squeeze over the lime juice and tear the coriander and basil to serve.
www.alpro.com

4 SUNDAY

5 MONDAY

6 TUESDAY

7 WEDNESDAY

8 THURSDAY

9 FRIDAY

10 SATURDAY

Blast from the past

Picked up a penguin

This photo is of me with my very best friend, Mr Percy Penguin. He was given to me when I was born by my favourite uncle. Percy accompanied me on all our family outings and holidays, as well as trips to the dentist and even a stay in hospital.

He came with me on my first day at school – however, the teacher informed me that penguins were not allowed and he would have to stay at home. I was rather miffed by this as he was a very well-behaved penguin.

One day, after visiting my grandmother, my Mum and I realised that I had left Percy on the number 81 bus. I was so upset that I cried myself to sleep. In the morning, the bus depot rang and told my mum that he had been found – much to my relief and Mum's!

I was so happy I told all my friends: "Sorry, I can't come out to play, I have to pick up a penguin." When asked how I managed to leave him on the bus, I replied: "I thought he had got off with me."

If Percy were travelling on buses now, he'd be old enough for a bus pass!
Meryl Ledbrooke, by email

No 1 this week

1983 Men at Work: Down Under
Recorded by Australian rock band Men at Work, Down Under was originally released in 1980 as the B-side to their first single Keypunch Operator. The hit song went to No.1 in their home country in December 1981 before spending four consecutive weeks at the top of the UK charts. Still a perennial favourite on Australian radio and TV, Men at Work were invited to play the song at the closing ceremony of the 2000 Summer Olympics in Sydney.

What a good idea

Not sure if an egg is fresh? Fill a bowl or glass with water and lower in the egg. A fresh egg sinks to the bottom and lies on its side. A week-old egg sinks but rests with the pointed end facing up. A 2-3 week old egg stands on its tip. A very old egg floats to the top.

Bizarre Britain

It's all rough and tumble in St Ives, Cornwall when silver ball hurling comes to town. An ancient form of rugby, locals boisterously hurl a silver ball at each other on the beach. Whoever wins the ball and returns it to the mayor on the steps of the St Ives Guidhall at the stroke of midday receives a silver coin.

Portrait of a star

RICHARD BURTON

BORN: **November 10, 1925**
DIED: **August 5, 1984**
KNOWN FOR: **Cleopatra, Who's Afraid of Virginia Woolf, Becket**
HE SAID: **"I rather like my reputation, actually, that of a spoiled genius from the Welsh gutter, a drunk, a womaniser; it's rather an attractive image."**

Recipe of the week

BAKEWELL TART WITH RHUBARB

Serves: 6   Preparation time: 15 mins
Cooking time: 35 mins

250g (9oz) puff pastry
4 tbsp Waitrose Rhubarb & Ginger Extra Fruity Preserve
100g (3oz) butter
100g (3oz) caster sugar
1 lemon grated and zested
1 medium egg beaten
100g (3oz) ground almonds
1 tsp of flaked almonds to decorate

1 Preheat the oven to 190°C/375°F/Gas Mark 5. Place a baking sheet in the oven to heat up. Roll out the pastry and use to line a 23cm (9in) pie plate. Prick all over with a fork. Spread the preserve over the base.

2 Cream the butter, sugar and lemon zest together until pale, then beat in the egg gradually. Fold in the ground almonds.

3 Spread the mixture over the jam leaving a border of about 4cm (1½in). Sprinkle with the flaked almonds.

4 Bake for 35-40 mins on the preheated sheet until the top of the tart is golden - cover the top with foil if it gets too brown.
www.waitrose.com

11 SUNDAY

12 MONDAY

13 TUESDAY

14 WEDNESDAY

15 THURSDAY

16 FRIDAY

17 SATURDAY

Blast from the past

Disposable income

Pocket money
when I was a kid,
Wasn't a penny
and certainly not a quid.
It was a shilling and you may think
This was a paltry sum each week for a kid,
But money was something we children
Didn't really seem to seek.
Every Saturday morning the lot
was spent in one go,
And if you're patient, how it went
I'll let you know.
Tuppence went on bus fares,
fourpence on our sweets,
A tanner went on Saturday morning pictures.
These were our only treats.
The Cisco Kid and Pancho were a Mexican duo
always doing good,
Like Davy Crockett, Sherwood's merry men
and Robin Hood.
We all loudly clapped and cheered our heroes
as they fought the villains of the plot,
And booed the baddies
when a comeuppance they got!
After that we couldn't wait
to get back home and play,
To mimic our silver-screen heroes
in every single way.
By now our riches had all been spent,
with nothing left to come,
But we didn't really mind at all as Saturdays
were such good fun.
Paul Lewis Kennedy, by email

No 1 this week

1961 Elvis Presley with The Jordanaires: Are You Lonesome Tonight?
Originally written in 1926, Are You Lonesome Tonight was Elvis Presley's 'comeback' single having completed two years' service in the US Army. The track was suggested by his manager Colonel Tom Parker who claimed it was his wife's favourite song. A month after its UK release it topped the singles chart and within three months had achieved sales of two million copies worldwide.

What a good idea

If you're having a sort out of your jewellery collection you may find necklaces have got tangled up together. For an easy way to untangle them, without breaking anything, sprinkle a little talc or a drop of almond oil onto the chain to ease out knots. Then use a pin to carefully unthread the chains from each other.

Bizarre Britain

As we tuck into our pancakes on Shrove Tuesday, the ladies of Olney, Buckinghamshire are racing with theirs as they compete in the world-famous Pancake Race. Dating back to 1445, it's thought the tradition began when a harassed housewife, hearing the shriving bell summoning her to confession, dashed to church still clutching her frying pan of pancakes.

Portrait of a star

ELIZABETH TAYLOR

BORN: **February 27, 1932**
DIED: **March 23, 2011**
KNOWN FOR: **Cleopatra, National Velvet, Cat on a Hot Tin Roof**
SHE SAID: **"The problem with people who have no vices is that generally you can be pretty sure they're going to have some pretty annoying virtues."**

Recipe of the week

YOGURT PANCAKES

Serves: 4 Preparation time:10 mins Cooking time: 4 mins

1 egg, beaten
150g (5oz) Greek-style yogurt
175ml (6floz) milk
1 tbsp melted butter, plus extra to grease
1 tsp caster sugar
½ tsp salt
150g (5oz) wholemeal flour
To serve:
20g (¾oz) blueberries
20g (¾oz) raspberries
Runny honey, to drizzle

1 Whisk the egg, yogurt, milk and melted butter together.

2 In a separate bowl, combine the sugar, salt and flour. Add the yogurt mixture to the dry ingredients and beat until smooth.

3 Lightly grease a frying pan and warm on a medium heat. Use 2 tbsp batter for each pancake and cook for 2 mins each side until golden brown.

4 Serve 2 pancakes each, with berries and runny honey.

Lakeland

18 SUNDAY

19 MONDAY

20 TUESDAY

21 WEDNESDAY

22 THURSDAY

23 FRIDAY

24 SATURDAY

Blast from the past

Young daredevils

We were made of tough stuff in the 1970s. These days, quite rightly, children have soft landings if they fall from climbing frames in play parks. It was different when I was young.

I remember dangling upside down from two climbing frames in our local park. One was shaped like a rocket, the other like an igloo. If I lost my grip, I fell on to concrete. Ouch! Many a scraped knee was had.

Once I fell off one of the swings as I went higher and higher, and ended up needing to have stitches above one eye. I still have a slight scar. It didn't put me off swings, though, and I still can't resist having a go!

Our slide was perilously high, with nothing around the top apart from fresh air. We used to hurtle down on our tummies, pretending to fly. I also loved the roundabout. I fancied myself as Olga Korbut so I would step from bar to bar as my friends made it go faster - and I never lost my balance.

Another favourite was a long horse with saddle seats which we pretended was Black Beauty. We hummed the theme tune as we made it 'gallop'.

Sharon Haston, Falkirk

No 1 this week

1981 Joe Dolce: Shaddap You Face
Joe Dolce's only hit single reached No.1 in 15 countries and sold an estimated six million copies worldwide. Dolce was born in 1947, the eldest of three children, to Italian-American parents and was inspired to write Shaddap You Face around the phrases he frequently heard his Italian grandparents say. Follow-up singles and albums never achieved the same success but Joe Dolce has continued to receive recognition as a poet and writer.

What a good idea

Call centres can sometimes bombard you with a catalogue of automated options to 'press 1 for this' and 'press 2 for that'. But if you don't know which option you'd like or simply want to speak to a human, try pressing 0 or # on your phone and you should be put through to a real person.

Bizarre Britain

By the light of the silvery moon, residents of Slaithwaite, west Yorkshire, take to the banks of the canal for a spot of moonraking. Derived from the centuries-old tale of smugglers who, caught pulling their illegal bounty from the water, told police they were raking the moon, residents now parade down along the water, floating a giant lantern and singing.

Portrait of a star

NATALIE WOOD

BORN: **July 20, 1938**
DIED: **November 1981**
KNOWN FOR: **West Side Story, Rebel Without a Cause, Miracle on 34th Street**
SHE SAID: **"The only time a woman really succeeds in changing a man is when he is a baby."**

Recipe of the week

POTATO AND MUSHROOM OMELETTE

Serves: 4 Preparation time: 20 mins
Cooking time: 20 mins

2 medium-sized potatoes, peeled and thinly sliced
1 tbsp olive oil
15g (½oz) butter
100g (3½oz) chestnut mushrooms, sliced
5 medium eggs
25ml (1floz) milk
2 tbsp chopped fresh parsley
Salt and pepper

1 For this recipe you need a 25cm (10in) non-stick frying pan.

2 Place the sliced potatoes into a pan of boiling water and cook for 5 mins, drain and set aside.

3 Add the olive oil and butter to the frying pan and cook the sliced mushrooms for about 5 mins.

4 While the mushrooms are cooking, preheat the grill. In a bowl, lightly whisk the eggs, milk, parsley and a little seasoning.

5 Add the potatoes to the mushrooms, arranging them evenly in the pan. Pour in the egg mixture and cook over a very low heat until the egg is setting around the edge. Then pop the pan under the grill and cook until set. Serve with fresh crisp salad.

www.lovepotatoes.co.uk

25 SUNDAY

26 MONDAY

27 TUESDAY

28 WEDNESDAY

1 THURSDAY

2 FRIDAY

3 SATURDAY

Blast from the past
Elton, Kiki and Biba

My first job, aged 16, was at Van Allan's store in Northumberland Street in Newcastle. I spent my first pay packet (£26!) on a pair of ankle strap black leather shoes and a new lipstick. How grown up I was!

We had first choice of the beautiful clothes to wear as our uniform and I wore them when I went out in the evening. My boyfriend (now my husband of forty years) told me I looked like a model.

We had our own hairdresser and Biba cosmetics counter in the store. Our very sophisticated supervisor looked like Joan Collins, beautifully made up and groomed. I aspired to be like her when I was older.

The store played lots of music throughout the day and I still smile when I hear Kiki Dee and Elton John singing Don't Go Breaking My Heart. I was in awe of one of the other girls on the staff who was dating a member of the band Goldie.

I stayed there for a couple of years, then went to work in an office nearer home, but I never forgot the glam days of Van Allan and, really, I should never have left!
Sylvia Lowery, by email

No 1 this week

1967 **Engelbert Humperdinck: Release Me**
Originally written in 1949 by two American country music artists, Eddie Miller and Robert Yount, Engelbert Humperdinck's version of the song was released after he sang it on Saturday Night at the London Palladium. Release Me has the distinction of being the best-selling single of 1967, holding the No.1 position for six weeks and keeping The Beatles' Penny Lane/Strawberry Fields Forever from reaching the top spot.

What a good idea

Some plastic packaging can be so tricky to get into, it can be easy to hurt your hands. But a clever way to open difficult packaging safely is to use a can opener. Just clamp it on to the edge and turn as usual. It's so much easier and safer than using scissors or a knife.

Bizarre Britain

You might think school PE lessons were the same Britain over - jabbing hockey sticks at one another on a freezing sports' field. But if you went to school in Rossall, Lancashire you would have learnt a sport so unique it's not played anywhere else. Rossall Hockey terrifyingly combines elements of rugby and hockey - think tackling with stick. Hairy stuff!

Portrait of a star

ELVIS PRESLEY

BORN: **January 8, 1935**
DIED: **August 16, 1977**
KNOWN FOR: **Viva Las Vegas, Love Me Tender, Jailhouse Rock**
HE SAID: **"Truth is like the sun. You can shut it out for a time, but it ain't goin' away."**

Recipe of the week

SAUSAGE AND POTATO CASSEROLE

Serves: 4 Preparation time: 15 mins
Cooking time: 15-20 mins

1 tbsp olive oil
2 onions, sliced
1 carrot, peeled and chopped
500g (1lb) Maris Piper/Rooster potatoes, cut into chunks
½ tsp chopped rosemary
1 tbsp Worcestershire sauce
250ml (8½floz) vegetable stock
1 tin of chopped tomatoes
1 tin of haricot beans, drained
1 tbsp chopped parsley
8 good quality sausages

1 Place a casserole dish over a medium heat, add half of the oil and cook the onions and carrot for 3-4 mins.
2 Add the potatoes, rosemary, Worcestershire sauce, stock, tomatoes, beans and parsley, stir and cook for 8 mins.
3 Fry the sausages separately until nicely browned then add to the casserole.
4 Cook with a lid on for 15 mins, stirring every so often to stop it sticking. This recipe is ideal for a slow cooker.
www.lovepotatoes.co.uk

4 SUNDAY

5 MONDAY

6 TUESDAY

7 WEDNESDAY

8 THURSDAY

9 FRIDAY

10 SATURDAY

Blast from the past

A stable career

I have always loved animals, especially dogs and horses, and my aim was to have a job connected with animals. An opportunity came along to work in a local hunting and show-jumping stables owned by the Oliver family who lived locally in Wendover.

When I started I was mostly mucking out and grooming the beautiful, spirited horses, but I loved it. Gradually, I progressed to exercising the horses each day. I stayed for about a year then found a job at another stables where the horses were used for filming at nearby Pinewood studios. This was a very interesting job, looking after all sorts of horses, ponies and donkeys.

Occasionally, we grooms were extras in some of the films. My friend Patricia stood in for Elizabeth Taylor during the filming of Cleopatra. We met quite a few celebrities in the Fifties and Sixties and I had the privilege of helping some actors to learn to ride. One of these was Roger Moore who needed to be able to ride for the Ivanhoe series on ITV.

After much pressure from my parents, I changed my career and joined the Royal Air Force, but I've always kept my love of horses.
Shirley Peters, by email

No 1 this week

1970 Lee Marvin: Wand'rin' Star
Written by Lerner and Loewe for the stage musical Paint Your Wagon in 1951. When the film of the musical was made in 1969, Lee Marvin took the role of prospector Ben Rumson and, although not a natural vocalist, sang all of his songs in the film. The film was a flop but the soundtrack became a success and Marvin's version of Wand'rin' Star became an unlikely No.1 single in the UK and Ireland. Unsurprisingly Marvin never released a follow-up single.

What a good idea

If you're having a wardrobe declutter and struggling to get rid of things, because you think you'll wear them again, try this trick. Turn all the hangers in your wardrobe the wrong way and only turn them back once you've worn the item. After six months, recycle any of the clothes on hangers still facing the wrong way.

Bizarre Britain

Every March, dozens of husbands throw their wives over their shoulders like a sack of spuds for the Wife Carrying Race in Dorking, Surrey. Believed to originate from Viking times when raiders carried away the wives of local men, today competitors race around a 380m course, negotiating hay bales and buckets of water. Anyone who drops their cargo is disqualified!

Portrait of a star

SAMMY DAVIS JR

BORN: **December 8, 1925**
DIED: **May 16, 1990**
KNOWN FOR: **Ocean's 11, Robin and The Seven Hoods**
HE SAID: **"Real success is not on the stage, but off the stage as a human being, and how you get along with your fellow man."**

Recipe of the week

POACHED EGGS WITH TOMATOES

Serves: 2 Preparation time: 10 mins Cooking time: 10 mins

2 peppers, sliced
1 red chilli, sliced
1 red onion, chopped
40g (1½ oz) fresh coriander
1 garlic clove, crushed
1 tsp paprika
Olive oil
1x400g (14oz) tin of tomatoes
4 eggs
150g (5oz) plain yogurt
1 tbsp of lemon juice
Handful chopped coriander
1 tbsp extra virgin olive oil

1 Fry the onion, peppers, garlic and half of the chilli, with 1 tsp paprika in a little olive oil for 4-5 mins then season. Add the tomatoes and cook for 3-4 mins.

2 Make 4 small round holes in the tomato mixture and crack an egg into each. Cover the pan with a lid and cook until the eggs are set.

3 Mix together the plain yogurt with the chopped garlic, lemon juice, half the chopped coriander and the extra virgin olive oil.

4 Serve the eggs and tomatoes with the yogurt mixture on the side, sprinkle over the rest of the coriander and chilli, and serve with toasted sourdough bread.

www.alpro.com

11 SUNDAY

12 MONDAY

13 TUESDAY

14 WEDNESDAY

15 THURSDAY

16 FRIDAY

17 SATURDAY

Blast from the past

Father was wrong

This is the story of my lovely in-laws, Lilian and Jerry.

Lilian left school in 1943 and worked in the town hall as a shorthand typist until she was seventeen and old enough to join the Wrens.

In 1946 she was posted to Haslemere and while she was waiting for a bus one day a large Canadian staff car pulled up and offered her a lift. As it was just after the war, she felt it was safe to accept. She and the Canadian soldier, Jerry, enjoyed chatting and started dating.

Within six weeks they decided to get married. Lilian's father was not pleased as his daughter was only eighteen and her boyfriend was nearly thirty. He wrote to Jerry's commanding officer to check that he didn't already have a family back home.

They married in July that year and in December went to live in Canada where Lilian gave birth to twin boys. But she was homesick for England and her large family so in 1950 they returned here.

They were happily married for sixty-one years and had four sons, ten grandchildren and two great grandchildren. It was a good job Lilian didn't listen to her father's advice!

Valerie Reilly, by email

No 1 this week

1958 Perry Como: Magic Moments
One of the first collaborations of songwriters Burt Bacharach and Hal David, Magic Moments was first published in 1958. Many versions have been recorded since but the biggest hit was Perry Como's single featuring the big band sound of the Mitchell Ayres' Orchestra and The Ray Charles Singers. The track spent eight weeks at No.1 and was one of Perry Como's biggest hits in the UK. Ronnie Hilton recorded a cover version the same year but only managed No.22 in the charts.

What a good idea

Eager knitter? Save yourself the hassle of tangled up yarn by grabbing the teapot! By placing the ball of wool in the teapot and feeding the strand of yarn through the spout, you shouldn't get knots and tangles. If you're knitting with multiple yarns, pop them in a colander and thread the yarn through the holes.

Bizarre Britain

Soggy dishcloths at the ready for some action-packed dwile flonking in Lewes, Sussex. An old pub game, dwile flonking involves lobbing a dishcloth fished out from a bucket of stale beer at pub regulars from the Lewes Arms. Whoever gets doused then has to take his or her revenge on the thrower.

Portrait of a star

TONY CURTIS

BORN: **June 3, 1925**
DIED: **September 29, 2010**
KNOWN FOR: **Some Like It Hot, Sweet Smell of Success, Spartacus**
HE SAID: **"I wouldn't be caught dead marrying a woman old enough to be my wife."**

Recipe of the week

HAZELNUT PLUM TART

Serves: 6-8 Preparation time: 15 mins
Cooking time: 40 mins

110g (4oz) rice flour
50g (2oz) cornflour
55g (2oz) ground hazelnuts
1 tsp cinnamon
110g (4oz) cold butter
75g (3oz) caster sugar
1 egg, beaten
450g (1lb) plums, stoned and quartered
2 tbsp soft light brown sugar
1 tsp cinnamon
Zest of 1 orange
1 tbsp ground hazelnuts
1 egg, beaten

1 Preheat the oven to 190°C/375°F/Gas Mark 5. Mix the rice flour, cornflour, 55g (2oz) ground hazelnuts, cinnamon and salt.

2 Rub the butter into the dry ingredients until it resembles breadcrumbs. Stir in the sugar. Pour in the beaten egg and bring the pastry together.

3 Roll out into a circle approximately 25cm (10in) wide and 3mm (1/8in) thick. Transfer to a roasting tin. Mix the plums, sugar, cinnamon, orange zest and 1 tbsp ground hazelnuts. Heap into the centre of the pastry, leaving a 5cm (2in) border.

4 Draw the edge of the pastry circle up over the fruit, pleating and pinching the pastry to form a leak-proof 'bowl'.

5 Brush the pastry with beaten egg and sprinkle over some sugar. Bake the tart for 40 mins.

The Genius Gluten-Free Cookbook by Lucinda Bruce-Gardyne (Vermilion, £14.99)

18 SUNDAY

19 MONDAY

20 TUESDAY

21 WEDNESDAY

22 THURSDAY

23 FRIDAY

24 SATURDAY

Blast from the past

High adventure

One day in 1971 my husband Peter was in the bathroom doing some decorating while our son Stephen was playing on the floor of the living room. He was 18 months old and just toddling.

I popped out for some coal, put it on the fire and then placed the shovel back. When I returned I was surprised to find Stephen was not there. It was only a small house with two rooms and a bathroom. There was a door to stop him going upstairs.

I called to see if he was with Peter but he wasn't. Then I heard a voice from above saying: "Me here, Mammy." There was Stephen up on the roof of the bathroom! In a matter of minutes he had climbed the ladder that had been left propped against the wall.

I had to climb up as fast as I could and got there just in time to grab him as he reached the edge of the roof. I carried the bairn down by one arm. By then Peter had come out to see what was happening. I handed Stephen over to his father, but didn't stop shaking for hours!

Doreen Duguid, Darlington

No 1 this week

1984 Lionel Richie: Hello

The memorable opening line: Hello, is it me you're looking for? would probably have been enough to propel this track to No.1 but, when combined with a distinctive video featuring an apparently blind student sculpting Lionel Richie's likeness in clay, success was guaranteed. The song and the video have since been parodied in various films and TV shows.

What a good idea

Want to give your old furniture a new lease of life? It may be as simple as rubbing out any scratches, scrapes and dints with a walnut. The oil in the nut moistens and helps fade away the dints and marks leaving your wooden furniture looking as good as new again.

Bizarre Britain

Equinoxes are always a time for unusual goings on and even in the capital you might spot something untoward on March 20 for the Spring Equinox. As day and night balance up for one day, the Druid Order at Tower Hill take to the streets in silence, wearing their white robes and scattering seeds to encourage a fruitful year ahead.

Portrait of a star

ERROL FLYNN

BORN: **June 20, 1909**
DIED: **October 14, 1959**
KNOWN FOR: **The Adventures of Robin Hood, They Died With Their Boots On**
HE SAID: **"The public has always expected me to be a playboy, and a decent chap never lets his public down."**

Recipe of the week

SPRING CHICKEN CASSEROLE

Serves: 4-6 Preparation time: 15 mins
Cooking time: 25 mins

500ml (17floz) chicken stock
8 free range chicken thighs, skinned
150g (5oz) baby carrots
500g (1lb) miniature new potatoes
4 Little Gem lettuce hearts, halved
155g (5½oz) peas
2 salad onions, thinly sliced
2 tbsp half-fat crème fraîche
4 tbsp chopped flat-leaf parsley

1 Place the stock and chicken in a large saucepan and bring to the boil. Cover and simmer for 10 mins, then add the carrots and potatoes. Simmer for a further 10 mins until the vegetables are almost cooked through.

2 Add the lettuce, peas and salad onions. Cover and cook for a further 4-5 mins until the peas are tender and the chicken is cooked through. Get a fork and test the juices by pricking the meat and making sure none of the juices are pink. Stir through the crème fraiche and parsley. Ladle into large soup bowls and serve.
www.waitrose.com

25 SUNDAY

26 MONDAY

27 TUESDAY

28 WEDNESDAY

29 THURSDAY

30 FRIDAY

31 SATURDAY

Blast from the past

Onward, Christian soldiers

In the early Sixties, my friend Cathy and I loved going on the GOOD FRIDAY MARCH (it was always spoken of in capital letters by church people as it was very important). It was important as the pivotal point of the Christian faith, but at the time for me and Cathy it was an opportunity for fun and adventure.

All the church people gathered in the town centre and walked from there to the church. Good Friday was a solemn and special day. All the shops and businesses were closed and there was a sombre air around the streets. Good Christians from all denominations marked this day by marching, sometimes with a leader carrying a cross.

Cathy and I, with lots of other children, tagged on with no idea of what it was all about except that it was a big occasion and some of the atmosphere was felt by us. The highlight was arriving at our own church and being given an orange by a kindly man in a warm black overcoat. After that, we went home and longed for Saturday when we could play as normal or, better still, Sunday when we could eat our Easter eggs.

Janet Lancefield

No 1 this week

1976 Brotherhood of Man: Save Your Kisses for Me
The UK's winning entry in the Eurovision Song Contest in 1976, Save Your Kisses for Me, became a surprise worldwide hit. The catchy jingle-like music, cutesy lyrics and simple dance routine all helped to secure maximum points from seven countries – beating the French into second place. And the song was propelled to No.1 and became the biggest-selling single of the year in the UK.

What a good idea

If your old kitchen knives are starting to look past their best and have gone rusty, give them a new lease of life by carefully plunging them into an onion three or four times. You should find that the rust then naturally just wipes off and your knives look like new.

Bizarre Britain

The Scottish Borders pay tribute every March to raiders, called 'border reivers' who lived on the Anglo-Scottish Border from the 13th to the 17th century with an annual Hawick Reivers Festival. Remembering the lawless clashes that went on between England and Scotland on these borders, the area now celebrates with torch-lit processions, falconry and livestock displays, re-enactments and banquets.

Portrait of a star

GENE KELLY

BORN: **August 23, 1912**

DIED: **February 2, 1996**

KNOWN FOR: **Singing In The Rain, An American In Paris, On The Town**

HE SAID: **"At 14 I discovered girls. At that time dancing was the only way you could put your arm around the girl. Dancing was courtship."**

Recipe of the week

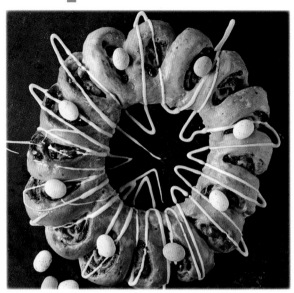

EASTER FRUIT GARLAND

Serves: 8 (2 slices each) Preparation time: 30-40 mins
Cooking time: 20-25 mins

500g (1lb) pack white bread mix
75g (3oz) sultanas
75g (3oz) currants
50g (2oz) glacé cherries
40g (1½oz) poppy seeds
50g (2oz) dark muscovado sugar
1 tsp mixed spice
15g (½oz) melted butter
50g (2oz) golden caster sugar
100g (3½oz) icing sugar

1 Make up the bread mix. Knead and prove. Roll out into a 50x30cm (20x12in) rectangle.

2 Mix together the sultanas, currants, glacé cherries, poppy seeds, sugar, mixed spice, and melted butter and spread over the dough, leaving a 2cm (½ in) border.

3 Roll up then curl into a circle, sealing the ends. Lift on to a baking sheet, then indent 16 slices with a knife. Twist so the cut surface lies upwards. Leave for 30-40 mins to rise.

4 Preheat the oven to 200°C/ 400°F/Gas Mark 6. Bake for 20-25 mins and leave to cool. Dissolve the caster sugar in 4 tbsp of boiling water and simmer for 2 mins. Paint over the garland. Combine the icing sugar with a little water to form a paste and drizzle over the garland. Decorate with mini chocolate eggs.

Lyle's Golden Syrup

1 SUNDAY

2 MONDAY

3 TUESDAY

4 WEDNESDAY

5 THURSDAY

6 FRIDAY

7 SATURDAY

Blast from the past

Henpecked then sacked!

After much pleading, when I was 13, I got the job of collecting the eggs at the farm where my dad was manager. This entailed collecting hundreds of eggs from several hen houses, cleaning them and putting them on trays in wooden boxes.

It was a dirty, smelly job and I often got pecked and chased by broody hens. I also got bitten by fleas so Mum made me disrobe in the porch on my return home.

By far the worst part, especially in bitter cold weather, was cleaning the poo off the eggs. As a special concession Dad let me have a Burco boiler in the shed so that I could take the chill off the water.

This job took hours, so on one freezing day I popped the eggs in the boiler and lifted them out one by one. The perfect solution - why hadn't I thought of it before?

A few weeks later Dad was fuming as the egg-packing station had found the eggs were coddled when they went through the testing machine. They couldn't understand why, but Dad guessed the reason. I was mortified when I lost my job and my fifteen shillings a week pay.
Margaret Rymer, Much Wenlock

No 1 this week

1964 The Beatles: Can't Buy Me Love
The Beatles' sixth single and their fourth UK No.1, Can't Buy Me Love was written by Paul McCartney. When pressed by US journalists to explain the lyrics he said the idea behind it was that material possessions were all very well but won't provide what we really need. The song was written and recorded in Paris where The Beatles were performing 18 days of concerts.

What a good idea

Egg boxes are a terrific, and cheap, gardening tool. Use your old egg box to sow seeds – just fill them up with soil and add a few seeds to each cell. Once the seedlings are big enough to plant out, cut up the egg box into their separate cells and plant each cell individually – cardboard and all – into the ground.

Bizarre Britain

Ewe wouldn't believe your eyes in north Devon, when the annual Big Sheep Grand National comes to town. Held on the same day as its equine cousin the British Grand National is going on at Aintree, the town of Bideford sees well-trained sheep take to a track, complete with knitted jockeys chivvying them on.

Portrait of a star

INGRID BERGMAN

BORN: **August 29, 1915**
DIED: **August 29, 1982**
KNOWN FOR: **Casablanca, Notorious, Spellbound**
SHE SAID: **"A kiss is a lovely trick designed by nature to stop speech when words become superfluous."**

Recipe of the week

CHICKEN AND JERSEY ROYAL BAKE

Serves: 4-6 Preparation time: 10 mins
Cooking time: 40-50 mins

4 tbsp olive oil
8 chicken thighs, skin on
600g (1lb 5oz) small Jersey Royal potatoes, scrubbed
2 heads garlic, cloves separated but not peeled
250g (9oz) Chantenay carrots, washed
8 sprigs thyme
125ml (4floz) chicken stock

1 Heat the oven to 190°C/375°F/Gas Mark 5. Heat half the oil in a large pan. Add the chicken and brown.
2 Remove and put the chicken and juices into a roasting tray.
3 Place on the hob and add the potatoes, garlic, carrots and herbs. Add the remaining oil and toss. Pour on the stock and heat until bubbling.
4 Remove from the heat and put in the oven. Cook for 40-50 mins.
www.jerseyroyals.co.uk

8 SUNDAY

9 MONDAY

10 TUESDAY

11 WEDNESDAY

12 THURSDAY

13 FRIDAY

14 SATURDAY

Blast from the past

The Goon Show

I joined the WRNS after leaving school in 1969. I learned how to march, salute, shine shoes and get the mess gleaming for inspections. This was followed by further training to be a weapon analyst before being drafted to my first naval establishment.

Soon after this a few of us were sent to a firing range in the north of Scotland for a week. To someone like me, who had never been further north than London, this was really exciting. The only way to get to our place of work was by helicopter. As we would be flying over water we had to wear something called a 'goon suit' for safety reasons. Looking at the photo, you can imagine the comments I received when trying it on in the mess!

After being dropped off by the chopper, two of us would spend the whole day in what was known as a quadrant hut, taking bearings of practice weapon flight paths. Two other WRNS were doing the same thing in another quadrant hut nearby.

On the way back, we would sometimes fly low over the fields, jump out and collect mushrooms for breakfast the next day!
Christine Barrow, by email

No 1 this week

1979 **Art Garfunkel: Bright Eyes**
Written by Mike Batt and performed by Art Garfunkel, Bright Eyes was used on the soundtrack of the animated film Watership Down. Helped by the haunting video of Hazel the rabbit and friends, the song stayed at No.1 for six weeks, selling more than one million copies. In 2000 ex-Boyzone singer Stephen Gately released a cover version which was used as the theme for a Watership Down TV series.

What a good idea

If junk mail is clogging up your email inbox, type 'unsubscribe' into your inbox search bar. This should bring up all the marketing emails you've received from various companies, allowing you to see whose mailing lists you're on. To remove yourself from any emails you no longer want to receive, click on the individual email and hit 'unsubscribe'.

Bizarre Britain

Thought dock leaves were just for nettle stings? In the Calder Valley in West Yorkshire, dock leaves are mixed together with nettles, oatmeal, onions, butter and seasoning to make a unique pie that's then put to the test in the World Dock Pudding Championships. First held in 1971, today dozens of ambitious cooks compete to make the best dock pudding.

Portrait of a star

JOAN CRAWFORD

BORN: **March 23, 1905**
DIED: **May 10, 1977**
KNOWN FOR: **Mildred Pierce, Whatever Happened to Baby Jane, The Women**
SHE SAID: **"I never go outside unless I look like Joan Crawford the movie star. If you want to see the girl next door, go next door."**

Recipe of the week

CHOCOLATE PRALINE CAKE

Serves: 8-10 Preparation time: 30 mins
Cooking time: 50-55 mins

100g (3½oz) whole blanched hazelnuts
175g (6oz) caster sugar
200g (7oz) dark chocolate (70 per cent cocoa), chopped
175g (6oz) unsalted butter, softened, plus extra for greasing
5 eggs separated
½ tsp salt

1 Preheat the oven to 180˚C/350°F/Gas Mark 4. Grease a 23cm (9in) cake tin. Roast the hazelnuts in the oven for 10 mins until golden. Blitz in a processor with 25g (1oz) of the sugar. Melt the chocolate.

2 Cream the butter and 100g (3½oz) sugar until pale and fluffy. Beat in the egg yolks one at a time, then add the melted chocolate and salt. Fold through the ground hazelnuts.

3 Reduce the temperature to 160˚C/300°F/Gas Mark 2. Whisk the egg whites until stiff, then whisk in the remaining 50g (2oz) sugar to form a meringue. Stir one third of the meringue into the chocolate mixture to slacken it, then fold in the rest. Bake for 50-55 mins.

4 Cool for 20 mins. Slice and serve with chocolate sauce and cream.
www.waitrose.com

15 SUNDAY

16 MONDAY

17 TUESDAY

18 WEDNESDAY

19 THURSDAY

20 FRIDAY

21 SATURDAY

Blast from the past

Limelight glow

As I was a bright, inquisitive child, my father taught me basic arithmetic, reading, writing and poetry appreciation from an early age. Unfortunately, when I started school my form teacher resented this, dismissing me and even refusing to use my first name! Although I loved acting and took dancing lessons, she always omitted me from the school productions.

One day a theatre troupe arrived at the school to stage a play. As a treat we didn't have to wear school uniform and I wore an eye-catching red dress. When they asked for a child to perform with them, I immediately volunteered and was chosen, despite the teacher pushing her own favourite forward. Imagine their surprise when I recited a verse from Tennyson's poem, The Lady of Shalott.

Afterwards, I took my curtain call with the actors who stood back so I could take a bow on my own. Later, I was the lead in school plays and won drama prizes. Although I didn't pursue an acting career, after graduating I became a theatre publicist, promoting professional performers.

But I'll never forget that first magical time when I basked in the glow of the limelight.
Charmaine Fletcher, by email

No 1 this week

1954 Doris Day: Secret Love
Who could forget Doris Day's emotional rendition of Secret Love in the film Calamity Jane? The single - recorded in one take with a live orchestra - was released in the US three weeks before the premier of the film. It reached No.1 twice in the UK for one week, on April 16, 1954 then again from May 7 for nine weeks. Doris Day was criticised for refusing to perform the song at the 26th Academy Awards, but Ann Blyth stepped in to sing the song at the ceremony.

What a good idea

Bread has lots of extra uses you might not have considered. One of our favourites is for getting rid of stains on wallpaper. Just rub over the stain with a piece of stale white bread and the mark should vanish. Bread also comes in handy for helping you safely pick up tiny fragments of broken glass from the floor.

Bizarre Britain

The Heffle Cuckoo Fair in East Sussex dates back to 1315 when Dame Heffle would release a cuckoo from her basket to herald the arrival of spring. Still held every year, the fair attracts hundreds of visitors who enjoy a variety of entertainment including Morris dancing, scarecrow displays, craft stalls and a traditional funfair.

Portrait of a star

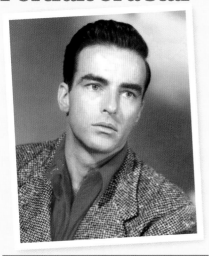

MONTGOMERY CLIFT

BORN: **October 17, 1920**
DIED: **July 23, 1966**
KNOWN FOR: **A Place In The Sun, From Here To Eternity, Raintree County**
HE SAID: **"Failure and its accompanying misery is for the artist his most vital source of creative energy."**

Recipe of the week

MINI SCONES

Makes: 12 Preparation time: 5 mins Cooking time: 8-10 mins

100g (3½oz) self-raising flour
25g (1oz) caster sugar
Pinch of salt
25g (1oz) unsalted butter, cubed
3 tbsp milk, plus extra to brush
Icing sugar, to dust

1 Preheat the oven to 220°C/425°F/Gas Mark 7. Grease and flour a baking sheet.
2 Sift the flour, sugar and salt into a bowl then rub in the butter until the mixture resembles breadcrumbs. Mix in the milk to form a soft dough.
3 Turn out on to a floured board and knead gently before patting out to 1.5cm (½in) thick. Cut into rounds using a 2.5cm (1in) pastry cutter and place on the prepared baking sheet.
4 Brush with milk and bake for 8-10 mins until well-risen and golden brown. Once cool, dust with icing sugar.
www.lakeland.co.uk

22 SUNDAY

23 MONDAY

24 TUESDAY

25 WEDNESDAY

26 THURSDAY

27 FRIDAY

28 SATURDAY

Blast from the past

A wartime welcome

In 1944 I was evacuated to Codnor, a small town in Derbyshire. I stayed with a lovely couple, Mr and Mrs Woolley and their son Hayden, who made me most welcome. Their address was 2 Meadow Avenue and at the end of their garden was a large meadow where there were cows that came up to the fence and let me stroke them.

The highlight of the week was Saturday evening when we all put on our best bib and tucker and went to the local working men's club. I would sit happily with a glass of lemonade watching couples dance to the music on a gramophone. One evening, Mrs Woolley decided to teach me to waltz. I felt so grown-up as I circled the dance floor, treading on her toes only once or twice.

On my ninth birthday she produced a lovely spread of food, despite the rationing, and invited six local children to my party. I was given a book entitled The Girls' Book of Heroines. When it was safe for me to return to my home in Morden, Surrey, I thanked them for taking care of me and said I would never forget their kindness - and I never have!
Pat Rose, Sidmouth

No 1 this week

1953 Frankie Laine: I Believe
American singer and actress Jane Froman originally commissioned the song I Believe because she was troubled by the outbreak of war in Korea. She asked songwriters to compose a tune that would 'offer hope and faith to the populace'. Frankie Laine's version spent 18 non-consecutive weeks at the top of the UK singles chart in 1953.

What a good idea

Don't pay for a fancy car air freshener when you can make your own. Fill a jam jar a quarter full of bicarbonate of soda. Sprinkle over five drops of your favourite essential oil. Put a piece of breathable fabric over the top of the jar and secure with an elastic band. Leave in your cup holder and shake occasionally.

Bizarre Britain

You better mind your head at Wath Festival, Yorkshire, where bun-throwing is an established tradition. Here the vicar, dressed up in historical costume, climbs up to the top of the church tower while a basket of bread is winched up to join him. As the clock strikes noon, a barrage of buns descends on the crowd below.

Portrait of a star

DAVID MCCALLUM

BORN: **September 19, 1933**
KNOWN FOR: **The Man From UNCLE, The Great Escape, Sapphire and Steel**
HE SAID: **"I think your life is governed not by the bricks or mortar around you, it's governed by who holds your hand and who spits in your eye."**

Recipe of the week

RASPBERRY AND APPLE FLAPJACKS

Serves: 10 Preparation time: 5 mins Cooking time: 20 mins

1 tbsp coconut oil
120g (4½oz) apple sauce
80ml (3 floz) Alpro oat original drink (or use milk instead)
1½ tbsp honey
1 tbsp cinnamon
125g (4½oz) oats
150g (5oz) raspberries

1 Preheat the oven to 180°C/350°F/Gas Mark 4. Grease a deep 15x15cm cake tin and set to one side. Melt the coconut oil in a large pan.

2 Mix with the apple sauce until well-blended and smooth. Add the Alpro or milk, honey, cinnamon and oats and mix well. Gently fold in the raspberries.

3 Pour the mixture into the tin and bake for 15-20 mins until golden brown. Remove from the oven and allow to cool before dividing the mixture into 10 equal pieces.
www.alpro.com

29 SUNDAY

30 MONDAY

1 TUESDAY

2 WEDNESDAY

3 THURSDAY

4 FRIDAY

5 SATURDAY

Blast from the past

Brighton Belle

This is a treasured photo of my mother, Lily, taken in 1942, wearing a fashionable fox fur, smart coat and hat and platform shoes. It was taken when she was 22... two years after her marriage to my father, Jeffery, a flight engineer in the RAF. He died on active service in 1943 when his Halifax bomber crashed, six months before I was born.

In 1947 we moved from the Midlands to a large house in Brighton where my grandmother rented out rooms to make ends meet. At the age of four I was sent away to boarding school, but this lasted only one month as my mother realised I was very unhappy there. After that, we had lots of fun times, eating ice cream on the pebbly beach or on the Palace Pier with its dodgem cars, rides and helter-skelters.

My mum remarried in 1950 and we moved to another house in Brighton. She had three more daughters, one of whom was put up for adoption, partly due to poor living conditions. That was in 1953 and, sadly, none of us ever saw my sister again.

Jacqueline Pomeroy, Brighton

No 1 this week

1970 Norman Greenbaum: Spirit in the Sky
Rolling Stone magazine named Spirit in the Sky No.333 in their list of the 500 Greatest Songs of All Time. The song, written and performed by Norman Greenbaum (who is generally considered to be a one-hit wonder), sold more than two million copies worldwide and has since been successfully re-recorded by Elton John, Doctor & The Medics and Gareth Gates.

What a good idea

Have you got a blocked plughole? Crush up two or three denture tablets and sprinkle down the plughole along with 200ml (7 fl oz) of white vinegar. Wait a few minutes for the denture tablets to do their magic and then rinse with hot water. Your drain should now be clear.

Bizarre Britain

Hastings plays host to a bizarre costumed parade as it celebrates the symbolic figure of Jack in the Green, the nickname given to chimney sweeps who wore green garlands as big as they were for the historic May Day processions. Locals now recreate this look in a parade ending with the slaying of Jack to release the spirit of summer.

Portrait of a star

GINA LOLLOBRIGIDA

BORN: **July 4, 1927**
KNOWN FOR: **Beat the Devil, Come September, The Hunchback of Notre Dame**
SHE SAID: **"We are all born to die – the difference is the intensity with which we choose to live."**

Recipe of the week

CUMIN-ROASTED BEETROOT, SQUASH AND CARROT WITH HERB SALAD

Serves: 4 Preparation time: 10 mins Cooking time: 35 mins

800g (1lb 9oz) butternut squash, peeled
4 raw beetroots, peeled
3 carrots, peeled
2-3 tbsp rapeseed or olive oil
2 tsp cumin seeds
Pinch dried chilli flakes
Salt and pepper
2 tbsp hazelnuts, roughly chopped
1 bag herb salad
100ml (3.5floz) coconut or natural yogurt
(low fat if you prefer)
1 lime

1 Preheat the oven to 200°C/400°F/Gas Mark 6. Chop the butternut squash, beetroot and carrot into bite-size chunks. Lay in a single layer in a baking tray and drizzle with half the oil.

2 Sprinkle with the cumin seeds and chilli and season well with the salt and pepper. Roast for 30 mins until the veg are softened and charred.

3 Meanwhile, toast the nuts in a dry frying pan then set aside.

4 Once tender, remove the vegetables from the oven. Tip the herb salad into a bowl and top with the roasted vegetables and hazelnuts.

5 Mix together the yogurt and zest of lime and drizzle over the salad. Drizzle the whole plate with the remaining oil, the juice of the lime and a good pinch of salt and pepper.

www.makemoreofsalad.com

6 SUNDAY

7 MONDAY

8 TUESDAY

9 WEDNESDAY

10 THURSDAY

11 FRIDAY

12 SATURDAY

Blast from the past

The heist

We get most of our values from our mums and dads and my two brothers and me were no exception. Especially from my mum who insisted on no cheating, no dishonesty, anywhere, ever. Well, almost never...

Growing up, I never felt poor, but I was aware that times weren't the easiest for us. So when I saw a chance to augment the family larder, I took it. I must have been about five. Seeing the grocer's van pull up outside and the driver climb out to deliver boxes of vegetables, I screwed up my courage, nipped into the back of the van, seized the biggest spud I could find and dashed triumphantly home with it.

"And where did you get that?" my mum asked in a voice that dashed any hopes of praise or reward. When I admitted the heist, she didn't hesitate: "Put it back, straightaway."

Panic stricken at the prospect of being collared by the grocer, I pleaded for mercy, but to no avail. "You should have thought of that first. We don't steal in this family."

Luckily, I managed to replace the potato undetected, but that lesson helped me stay on the straight and narrow thereafter.
David Simmonds, Penarth

No 1 this week

1978 Boney M: Rivers of Babylon
Germany-based disco band Boney M's cover version of Rivers of Babylon is one of the top ten all-time best-selling singles in the UK. Originally written by a Jamaican reggae group called The Melodians the lyrics are adapted from the texts of Psalms 19 and 137 in the Bible. The song was initially banned in Jamaica because the words of the Psalms were altered to reference the band's Rastafarian beliefs. For their cover version Boney M reinstated the biblical texts.

What a good idea

If old feather pillows seem past their best, it may be that they need a bath. Pop the pillow into a bath of warm water and mild detergent. Then step into the bath and tread on the pillow. After a minute, rinse out with clean, warm water and spin one pillow at a time in the washing machine. Dry naturally.

Bizarre Britain

There's a worm at the bottom of the garden... but the wormcharmers of Blackawton, Devon are sure to bring them up to say 'hello' for the International Festival of Wormcharming that's been going on since 1983. Locals use different liquids – sampled first by the judges - to tempt the wrigglies up and win the title of top wormcharmer.

Portrait of a star

JAMES STEWART

BORN: **May 20, 1908**
DIED: **July 2, 1997**
KNOWN FOR: **It's A Wonderful Life, Rear Window, Vertigo, Harvey**
HE SAID: **"Well, I think one of the main things that you have to think about when acting in the movies is to try not to make the acting show."**

Recipe of the week

SKINNY BLUEBERRY MUFFIN

Serves: 10 Preparation time: 15 mins Cooking time: 30 mins

300g (11oz) self-raising flour, sieved
1 tsp baking powder, sieved
1 tsp bicarbonate of soda, sieved
175g (6oz) low-calorie sugar
100ml (4 floz) rapeseed oil
2 eggs
100ml (4 floz) soya milk
2 apples, peeled and grated
250g (9oz) punnet fresh blueberries or use frozen

1 Preheat the oven to 200°C/400°F/Gas Mark 6.
2 Mix together the flour, baking powder, bicarbonate of soda and sugar.
3 Beat in the oil, eggs and soya milk, then stir in the grated apple and a third of the blueberries.
4 Spoon the mixture evenly between 10 paper muffin cases then top each one with remaining blueberries, pushing them slightly into the mixture.
5 Bake in the oven for about 25-30 mins until risen and golden.
www.canderel.co.uk

13 SUNDAY

14 MONDAY

15 TUESDAY

16 WEDNESDAY

17 THURSDAY

18 FRIDAY

19 SATURDAY

Blast from the past

Caught redhanded

I remember my parents going to the pictures when I was five. I was supposed to be asleep, but could hear Mum giving my two big brothers, already in bed, instructions. "See your sister's all right, don't keep the light on, don't let Pluto into your bed and see that you're asleep by the time we get back."

Little did she know that I was listening, that the dog was already in my brother's big bed and that they were furiously trying to hold down his wagging tail. As Dad shut the front door, the fun began. The boys fetched me and we all practised falling on to their bed, keeping our legs straight and tipping forwards without bending our bodies. I always lost that game as I couldn't help crumpling in the middle, earning scornful comments. Then the highlight of the evening (well, it was for the boys, anyway) – grabbing Mum's best satin cushions and sliding up and down the highly polished linoleum in the hallway.

My job was to keep watch. On this particular occasion, I didn't notice through the net curtains two figures coming up the garden path. Then above the din, we heard a key in the lock. The door opened and we were caught red-handed!
Olive Davies, by email

No 1 this week

1958 Connie Francis: Who's Sorry Now?
First published in 1923, Who's Sorry Now? was featured in the Marx Brothers' film A Night in Casablanca. It became a major hit for Connie Francis who, having recorded 20 tracks and achieving no chart success, was on her last chance with record company bosses at MGM. Connie's father suggested the track because he was convinced it would have crossover appeal with older listeners and teenagers. Initially the song looked to be another flop until it was picked up and championed by Dick Clark on his TV show American Bandstand.

What a good idea

Get your closet smelling fresh and clean with the help of your socks! For a simple DIY air freshener for your wardrobe, fill a clean sock with some dry coffee grounds, tie the top of it and hang in your wardrobe or cupboard. The coffee will absorb any musty smells.

Bizarre Britain

This Whit Sunday it'll be raining bread and cheese in St Briavels, Gloucestershire. In a tradition that goes back to the 12th century, the vicar blesses a loaf and batch of cheese - to make it a lucky charm - before chucking it at the gathered crowds waiting to catch the bounty in upturned umbrellas.

Portrait of a star

LORETTA YOUNG

BORN: **January 6, 1913**
DIED: **August 12, 2000**
KNOWN FOR: **The Bishop's Wife, The Call of the Wild, The Stranger**
SHE SAID: **"If you want a place in the sun, you have to expect a few blisters."**

Recipe of the week

MUSHROOM, SPINACH AND EGG BREAKFAST BAKE

Serves: 4 Preparation time: 10 mins Cooking time: 30 mins

3 tbsp olive oil
½ small red onion, chopped
300g (10½oz) chestnut mushrooms, halved if small, quartered if large
1 small leek finely sliced
100g (4oz) of spinach
Salt and pepper to taste
4 slices crusty bread
5 large eggs
130ml (¼pt) milk
150g (5oz) finely-grated parmesan

1 Brush 1 tbsp of oil into a 23x32cm (9x13in) baking dish.
2 Heat the remaining olive oil in a large frying pan and cook the onions until soft. Stir in the mushrooms and leeks and cook until softened.
3 Stir in the spinach and cook until wilted. Remove from heat and set aside to cool.
4 Arrange bread slices in a single layer in a baking dish. Layer bread with mushroom mixture. Crack the eggs on top. Season with salt and pepper. Pour milk evenly over top and sprinkle with the cheese.
5 Bake until the eggs are set, about 25-30 mins.
www.justaddmushrooms.com

20 SUNDAY

21 MONDAY

22 TUESDAY

23 WEDNESDAY

24 THURSDAY

25 FRIDAY

26 SATURDAY

Blast from the past

Ring-a-ding-ding!

We were married in 1959 in Little Common in Sussex. Our best man said he didn't want to be responsible for keeping the ring so my fiancé's younger brother said he would deliver it safely on the day.

Our wedding guests were travelling to Cooden Beach Station by train from where they were met by cars to take them to our village.

When I arrived at the church, I was told that my husband's family weren't there although they had been seen on the train. The chauffeur drove me off again on two circuits but there was still no sign of them.

The registrar suggested we should borrow a ring, so my sister-in-law lent us hers and the service began. One of the five priests attending stood at the back of the church to look out for my future in-laws. Just as we got to the exchange of rings, there was a flurry at the door as the late guests arrived. They had travelled on to Bexhill by mistake and caught a bus back to our village.

The priest uttered some very unpriestly words and the rings were swopped at the last moment. Fifty-eight years later we still laugh at the memory.
Jennifer Stanley, Croydon

No 1 this week

1956 Ronnie Hilton: No Other Love
No Other Love was written by the legendary duo Rodgers and Hammerstein for the musical Me and Juliet. Richard Rodgers originally composed the music for the NBC TV series Victory at Sea and collaborated with lyricist Oscar Hammerstein to put words to the melody for the 1953 stage show. Previously recorded by Ella Fitzgerald, Perry Como and Bing Crosby it was English singer Ronnie Hilton who took the song to the top of the UK charts.

What a good idea

Did you know the secret to a happy garden could be in your fridge? Once you've finished with your eggs, use the shells, ground up, to sprinkle over plants to give them a much-appreciated calcium boost. Old plastic milk bottles, cut in half will also make great cloches to protect tender plants from bugs and bad weather.

Bizarre Britain

Forget the pressure of a Slimming World weigh-in. That's nothing compared to the weighing-in ceremony of the Mayor of High Wycombe who must publicly take to the scales every year. If they weigh more than last year, they'll be booed - historically their indulgence was considered to be at the taxpayer's expense - while a weight-loss raises cheers.

Portrait of a star

JOHN WAYNE

BORN: **May 26, 1907**
DIED: **June 11, 1979**
KNOWN FOR: **True Grit, The Man Who Shot Liberty Valance, The Searchers, Rio Bravo**
HE SAID: **"I would like to be remembered, well . . . the Mexicans have a phrase, "Feo fuerte y formal". Which means he was ugly, strong and had dignity."**

Recipe of the week

PLUM BAKEWELL

Serves: 8 Preparation time: 15 mins Cooking time: 30 mins

2 tbsp raspberry jam
2 eggs
400g (14oz) caster sugar
20g (¾oz) almonds
1 tsp vanilla extract
Zest of half a lemon
8 plums
Handful of flaked almonds
1 tbsp icing sugar

1 Preheat the oven to 180°C/350°F/Gas Mark 4. Put a 21cm (8in) butter pastry tart on to a baking sheet and spoon in the raspberry jam, spreading it evenly over the base.

2 Beat together the eggs, caster sugar, almonds, vanilla extract and lemon zest. Spoon into the tart case and spread it out over the jam.

3 Pit and halve the plums and place on top. Sprinkle over the flaked almonds and bake in the oven for 25-30 mins, until the filling is set and golden. Cool for about 20 mins, then serve, sprinkled with icing sugar.
www.beautifulcountrybeautifulfruit.com

27 SUNDAY

28 MONDAY

29 TUESDAY

30 WEDNESDAY

31 THURSDAY

1 FRIDAY

2 SATURDAY

Blast from the past

My little green desk

This photo was taken in the summer of 1968. The desk was wooden and painted green. The hinged top lifted up for me to keep my pens and books in. I loved that desk which was usually in my bedroom, not out in the garden.

Although I was only five, I could read and write quite well. I would spend hours writing, pretending I was grown up. I used to buy Ladybird books with my pocket money. I loved the history series, especially the ones about the kings and queens of England. I thought the drawings in these books were wonderful and I'd read them from cover to cover. It looks like one of my comics on the desk, maybe the one I had called Teddy Bear.

Although I used to copy the pages of my Ladybird books to practise my handwriting, I didn't grow up to be a writer. I worked in Barclays Bank for 24 years and these days I work in the same school that I attended as a pupil. From the second-floor room I occupy at the school, I can just see the house we lived in when I was a girl. I haven't moved very far in 50 years!
Toni Robarts, by email

No 1 this week

1966 Rolling Stones: Paint It Black
The Rolling Stones third No.1 single in the UK, Paint It Black stayed at the top of the charts for ten weeks. Written by Mick Jagger and Keith Richards the song's lyrics, for the most part, describe bleakness and depression. Bassist Brian Jones was responsible for the inclusion of a sitar instrumental because he'd become bored with playing conventional guitar melodies.

What a good idea

To stretch out new shoes, put on a pair of socks and then your shoes. Use a hairdryer to gently heat the tight areas for a few seconds, while wiggling and stretching your feet inside. Keep your shoes on as they cool down, before removing your socks (if needed) and testing out your newly-stretched shoes for size.

Bizarre Britain

Every year the county of Rutland hosts the World Championship of Nurdling. For the uninitiated, nurdling is a game which dates back to the Middle Ages and involves throwing old pennies into a drilled hole in a wooden seat. Taking place at The Jackson Stops in Stretton, locals compete to be crowned the 'Best Tosser'.

Portrait of a star

BETTE DAVIS

BORN: **April 5, 1908**
DIED: **October 6, 1989**
KNOWN FOR: **All About Eve, Now Voyager, Whatever Happened to Baby Jane**
SHE SAID: **"I'd marry again if I found a man who had fifteen million dollars, would sign over half to me, and guarantee that he'd be dead within a year."**

Recipe of the week

SMOKED HADDOCK FISH CAKES

Serves: 4 Preparation time: 25 mins Cooking time: 40 mins

750g (1½lb) potatoes, peeled and quartered
500g (1lb) skinned smoked haddock
50g (2oz) butter, melted
1x85g (3oz) pack watercress, finely chopped
2 eggs, beaten
3 tbsp oil
200g (8oz) natural dry breadcrumbs

1 Boil the potatoes until soft, drain well and mash. Leave to cool. Steam the smoked haddock for 8-10 mins. Cool and flake, removing all the bones.

2 Stir the haddock flakes into the mashed potatoes. Add the melted butter and watercress and form into eight cakes. Chill for 15 mins.

3 Dip each cake into the beaten eggs, then the breadcrumbs and fry gently in hot oil for 3 mins each side.

4 Place on a baking tray in the oven and cook for 20 mins at 220°C/425°F/Gas Mark 7, turning halfway through. Serve with a crisp, mixed leaf and watercress salad.
www.watercress.co.uk

3 SUNDAY

4 MONDAY

5 TUESDAY

6 WEDNESDAY

7 THURSDAY

8 FRIDAY

9 SATURDAY

Blast from the past

Knickerbocker glory

My first experience of stardom has led me to avoid the limelight from that day to this. At the age of seven I was chosen to be the flower queen in our annual gala parade.

The week before my big day a visit to the dentist resulted in my four front teeth (the top ones) going to the tooth fairy, despite my mother's fervent pleas. She and I agreed that if I was asked to smile during the gala I should keep my mouth firmly shut.

But worse was to come. When the big day arrived I was seated on my decorated float with all my little attendants around me when I felt a ghastly 'pop' and realised the elastic in my knickers had burst.

Forgetting that the elastic in the legs would prevent my knickers from falling down around my ankles, I gripped them firmly through my dress as I performed all my duties and curtsies. The elegant performance I had carefully rehearsed went down the drain!

And then, to top it all, the 'gemstone' in the front of my crown fell off... So much for my brief moment of glory!

Liz Fiddler, by email

No 1 this week

1966 Frank Sinatra: Strangers In The Night
Bert Kaempfert is credited with writing the music for Strangers In The Night under the name Beddy Bye as part of the instrumental score for the film A Man Could Get Killed. But Frank made it his own with his scat improvisation of the melody with the syllables 'doo-be-doo-be-doo' as the song fades to the end. Sinatra apparently hated the song but it gave him his first No.1 hit in 11 years and won him a Grammy Award.

What a good idea

If your garden is looking like it wants a drink but you don't fancy lugging a heavy watering can around, try using a milk bottle instead. Punch holes into the lid of a large plastic milk bottle, screw the lid back on and water away. You can adapt the size of holes to suit the type of plants you're watering.

Bizarre Britain

Shinpads at the ready for a 400-year-old shin-kicking contest that forms a major part of the Cotswold Olimpicks. Set up by poet and lawyer Robert Dover around 1612 this wacky rural challenge features events like hammer throwing, wheelbarrow-racing, hitting people with a wooden sword and wrestling by kicking your opponent's shins using steel-capped shoes. Ouch!

Portrait of a star

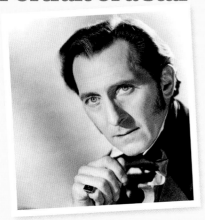

PETER CUSHING

BORN: **May 26, 1913**
DIED: **August 11, 1994**
KNOWN FOR: **The Curse of Frankenstein, Horror of Dracula, Star Wars: Episode IV**
HE SAID: **"Who wants to see me as Hamlet? Very few. But millions want to see me as Frankenstein so that's the one I do."**

Recipe of the week

ASPARAGUS AND HAM ROLLS

Serves: 6 Preparation time: 15 mins
Cooking time: 15-20 mins

1x320g (11oz) sheet ready-rolled all-butter puff pastry
120g (4oz) garlic & herb soft cheese
100g (3½oz) fine asparagus spears
3 slices Parma ham, cut in half lengthways
1 egg, beaten
1 tbsp Parmesan cheese, finely grated

1. Preheat the oven to 200°C/400°F/Gas Mark 6. On a floured surface cut the pastry into 6 equal squares.
2. Spread a sixth of the soft cheese diagonally along the centre of each square. Take a sixth of the asparagus spears and wrap them in one of the pieces of ham. Lay the ham-wrapped asparagus over the soft cheese. Pull the two opposite corners of pastry over the filling and brush the pastry with the beaten egg to seal. Repeat with the other squares, then sprinkle the rolls with the Parmesan.
3. Bake on a lined baking sheet for 15-20 mins, until the pastry is crisp and golden. The rolls can be served warm or at room temperature. They can be kept in the fridge for up to 2 days.

Cath Kidston TEATIME: 50 Cakes and Bakes for Every Occasion. Quadrille. RRP: £15

10 SUNDAY

11 MONDAY

12 TUESDAY

13 WEDNESDAY

14 THURSDAY

15 FRIDAY

16 SATURDAY

Blast from the past

A permanent wave

There can't be many people who had their first visit to the hairdresser at the age of just ten days. My mum, Margaret, brought me home from hospital on a June afternoon in 1956 and opened a hair salon in the front room of our home on the same day. Sixty years later I celebrated my 'big' birthday there as she is still working and has many of the same clients.

I grew up in the era of shampoos and sets, perms and finger-waves. It wasn't unusual to have 40 clients in one day and mum took very few breaks. In 1962, my brother, Adrian, was born in the upstairs bedroom, shortly after Mum had styled the midwife's hair!

As a teenager, I used to help in the salon. The tips I earned were added to my 50p wages and went towards buying the latest Seventies fashions from Chorley Market. Now that I am retired from a career in education, I help Mum when she is busy and enjoy chatting to clients who have become friends and regale me with tales of my childhood. And in return, I get a free hair-do if I'm lucky!

Linda Sherlock, Chorley

No 1 this week

1956 Pat Boone: I'll Be Home
Originally a hit for the band The Flamingos, Pat Boone's cover of I'll Be Home was the best-selling single of the year in the UK. After Elvis, Pat Boone was by far the most popular and successful singer of the period, selling over 45 million records in the Fifties and Sixties and appearing in 12 Hollywood films. Pat Boone still holds the record for spending 220 consecutive weeks on the US Billboard charts with one or more songs each week.

What a good idea

The last thing you want when you arrive on holiday is to discover your creams and products have leaked all over your clothes. Prevent this by wrapping a piece of cling film over the top before replacing the lid. This way, if the lid opens the cling film should prevent any leaks.

Bizarre Britain

Running a race in bed might seem like a nice idea, but it's a gruelling challenge for the hundreds who take part in The Great Knaresborough Bed Race. First staged in 1966, groups push elaborately dressed beds around the town's cobbled streets along a 2.4 mile course, ending with competitors taking an icy swim in the River Nidd.

Portrait of a star

JAMES DEAN

BORN: **February 8, 1931**
DIED: **September 30, 1955**
KNOWN FOR: **Rebel Without a Cause, Giant, East of Eden**
HE SAID: **"If a man can bridge the gap between life and death... I mean, if he can live on after his death, then maybe he was a great man."**

Recipe of the week

MUSHROOM BURGERS

Serves: 4 Preparation time: 15 mins Cooking time: 10 mins

250g (9oz) chestnut mushrooms, wiped and roughly chopped
70g (3oz) butter beans
70g (3oz) chickpeas
1 medium onion, finely diced
1 tbsp fresh parsley, finely chopped
2 cloves garlic, finely diced
1 heaped tsp paprika
1 medium egg yolk
2 slices wholemeal bread, cut into small chunks
Sea salt and black pepper
Sunflower oil

1 Put all the ingredients except the sunflower oil into a food processor, season with salt and pepper then process until well mixed and still a bit chunky.
2 Divide the mixture into 4 portions and roll into round patties. Chill in the fridge for 15 mins until firm.
3 Brush with the sunflower oil and then barbecue or fry for 5 mins on each side.
4 Serve on toasted brioche buns with rocket, sliced tomato and soft cheese with garlic and herbs.
www.aldi.co.uk

17 SUNDAY

18 MONDAY

19 TUESDAY

20 WEDNESDAY

21 THURSDAY

22 FRIDAY

23 SATURDAY

Blast from the past

Devon days

In the 1940s my family lived ten miles away from my favourite seaside resort, Dawlish Warren in Devon. We travelled there by steam train from Exeter, bringing our own sandwiches and drinks. My father knew a carpenter who made us a wooden beach hut that contained a table and benches to sit on. It had a Primus stove to boil a kettle and miniature cooker fuelled by Calor Gas. Neighbours and relatives often came along as well and on a dull day the adults enjoyed a game of cards in the beach hut.

The photo shows my older sister and me wearing the swimsuits that my mother knitted for us. She was usually left holding our shoes and clothing. There were rock pools to explore with mussels and crabs and shellfish to catch with a net. At the age of eight I learned to swim in the sea which I loved even though my lips were often blue with cold when I returned to dry off in the comfort of the beach hut!

At the end of the season all the beach-hut owners had a get-together. There was a firework display and a supper of fish and chips supplied by the local café.

Sheila Mills, Minehead

No 1 this week

1963 Gerry & The Pacemakers: I Like It
The second single by Liverpudlian group Gerry and the Pacemakers, I Like It reached No.1 on June 20, 1963. Gerry Marsden and his band had worked the same Liverpool and Hamburg circuit as their Mersybeat rivals The Beatles and were signed by pop impresario Brian Epstein and produced by George Martin. Their follow up single, a cover of the Rogers and Hammerstein show tune You'll Never Walk Alone, quickly became the anthem of Liverpool FC.

What a good idea

The warmer weather can leave tough perspiration stains on white shirts. But it's easy to get your shirt gleaming and fresh again, simply by reaching for the painkillers. For a cheap and easy cleaning solution, crush two aspirin into 100ml of warm water. Then soak the stained area for two to three hours and throw in the wash as you would usually.

Bizarre Britain

You'll need some strong tootsies to participate in the annual Fenny Bentley World Toe Wrestling Championship in Derbyshire. In a tradition that began in the Seventies, competitors have to sit on the floor and lock big toes, attempting to wrestle their opponents' feet. All competitors must pass a rigorous toe inspection before they can step up to the 'toedium'.

Portrait of a star

BOB HOPE

BORN: **May 29, 1903**
DIED: **July 27, 2003**
KNOWN FOR: **Road to Rio, My Favourite Brunette, The Cat and the Canary**
HE SAID: **"I have seen what a laugh can do. It can transform almost unbearable tears into something bearable, even hopeful."**

Recipe of the week

STRAWBERRY TRIFLE WITH PIMMS

Serves: 6 Preparation time: 25 mins Chilling time: 2 hours

4 trifle sponges
350g (12oz) of sliced strawberries
2 tbsp sugar
4 tbsp of Pimms
425g (15oz) of reduced-fat custard
200ml (7floz) of double cream
150g (5oz) of low-fat natural yogurt
Grated zest from half an orange and half a lemon

1. Break the trifle sponges into pieces and arrange in a single layer in the base of a 1.2 litre (2pt) glass dish.
2. Arrange the strawberries on top, sprinkle with sugar. Spoon over the Pimms.
3. Pour the custard over the top of the fruit and spread into an even layer.
4. Whip the double cream, then fold in yogurt. Mix in the grated zest.
5. Spoon the cream mixture over the custard and chill until required.
6. Decorate with strawberries and pansy flowers or lemon and orange rind curls made with a zester.

Pimms

24 SUNDAY

25 MONDAY

26 TUESDAY

27 WEDNESDAY

28 THURSDAY

29 FRIDAY

30 SATURDAY

Blast from the past

I was in the dark!

When I was eight years old my mother woke me at 2.30am on March 25, 1943. She told me to get my grandmother.

I was given a candle under a jam jar to guide me. I walked along the road to a house a couple of doors away from ours. Through the letterbox I pulled a piece of string that held my aunt's key. Then I opened the door and climbed in the pitch dark.

I woke my aunt and we went back to my house, round the back, down the garden to the pathway that ran between our garden and the farm at the bottom. Over the stile we climbed – the candle had gone out by this time! A few steps took us to the plank over the stream, up a steeply sloping garden, through the trees to my grandmother's house where I was able to go back to sleep.

I remember nothing more until I woke the following morning to find to my complete surprise that I had a baby brother!

This photo is of me and my sister taken on Portsmouth Navy Day in 1956 when we were in our early twenties.
Hilda Dalkin, by email

No 1 this week

1960 Eddie Cochran: Three Steps to Heaven Three Steps to Heaven became a posthumous UK No.1 hit for Cochran following his death in a car accident in April 1960. It was recorded three months previously and featured the guitarist and drummer from Buddy Holly's Crickets. David Bowie used the guitar riff in his 1971 song Queen Bitch and Showaddywaddy's 1975 cover version was also a hit, reaching No.1 in Ireland and No.2 in the UK charts.

What a good idea

Do you want a simple way to make your lovely bakes last longer? Then try storing your favourite cake alongside an apple cut in half. The apple will cleverly stop your cake from drying out and extend the shelf-life significantly, meaning your cake will stay at its best for much longer.

Bizarre Britain

You very well might end up with egg on your face if you head to Swaton, Lincolnshire where the World Egg Throwing Championship is held every year. Whether you like your eggs fried, scrambled or otherwise, you'll find them heading towards you in relays, from trebuchets and even in a Russian egg roulette.

Portrait of a star

CLARK GABLE

BORN: **February 1, 1901**
DIED: **November 16, 1960**
KNOWN FOR: **Gone With the Wind, It Happened One Night, The Misfits**
HE SAID: **"The things a man has to have are hope and confidence in himself against odds, and sometimes he needs somebody, his pal or his mother or his wife or God, to give him that confidence."**

Recipe of the week

HALLOUMI KEBABS

Serves: 4 Preparation time: 15 mins Barbecue time: 10 mins

225g (8oz) halloumi
4 large or 8 medium chestnut mushrooms
1 red pepper, deseeded and chopped
1 courgette, chopped
2 packs sundried tomato and garlic couscous
½ tbsp fresh coriander, finely chopped
Black pepper
50ml (2floz) olive oil

1 Preheat the grill. Cut the halloumi into 12 chunks. If using larger mushrooms, cut into quarters or into halves. Use four mushroom pieces and three halloumi chunks on each skewer.
2 Brush oil over them, season and grill for about 10 mins.
3 Sauté the pepper and courgette in the remaining olive oil until just browned.
4 Prepare the couscous as per the packet instructions, then stir through the peppers, courgettes and coriander. Serve the kebabs on a bed of couscous.
www.aldi.co.uk

1 SUNDAY

2 MONDAY

3 TUESDAY

4 WEDNESDAY

5 THURSDAY

6 FRIDAY

7 SATURDAY

Blast from the past

Love forever true

This photo is of Lawrence and me on our wedding day. We met when we were both fifteen. He was tall and good-looking with a cheeky sense of humour. We started going out regularly and within a very short time we knew we were meant for each other.

Six months later, Lawrence's family moved 40 miles away. There were no mobile phones in those days and most families didn't even have a phone in the house. So Lawrence and I wrote to each other. Our parents allowed us to meet up and stay at each other's houses every weekend - sleeping in separate beds, of course!

Four years later we were married and our happiness was complete. Words couldn't express the joy of being together at long last. A few people still said it wouldn't last. Married at nineteen - what were the chances?

After a few years I became pregnant but sadly miscarried. Doctors told us that I couldn't carry a baby. We bravely accepted this devastating news and had many happy times, despite being childless. Although we have had our ups and downs, as most couples do, in 2017 we celebrated our 55th wedding anniversary.
Olga Rose, West Midlands

No 1 this week

1972 Donny Osmond: Puppy Love
Originally written by Paul Anka for the American actress and singer Annette Funicello, whom he was dating at the time, Puppy Love reached No.33 in the UK chart in 1960. Twelve years later Donny Osmond's cover version was his third solo single and his first No.1 in the UK. What sold the record was Donny's emotional delivery of the line, 'Someone help me, help me, help me please'. Teen girls everywhere swooned while young men looked on bemused.

What a good idea

Make the bed easier: Turn your duvet cover inside out and lay it over the bed. Put the duvet on top, lined up with the edges. Roll up the duvet and cover together from the closed top edge of the duvet to make a sausage shape. Pull the open end over the duvet sausage and do it up. Finally unroll.

Bizarre Britain

Hay we go! First started in the Seventies as a bet between two blokes, the Oxenhope Straw Race in West Yorkshire sees teams of locals carrying a bale of straw around a course while drinking a pint of beer in each of the five pubs en-route. To date, the race has raised more than £250,000 for charity.

Portrait of a star

CARY GRANT

BORN: **January 18, 1904**
DIED: **November 29, 1986**
KNOWN FOR: **North by Northwest, Charade, His Girl Friday, Notorious**
HE SAID: **"My formula for living is quite simple. I get up in the morning and I go to bed at night. In between, I occupy myself as best I can."**

Recipe of the week

CAMEMBERT APPLE TARTS

Makes: 12 Preparation time: 25 mins Cooking time: 25 mins

25g (1oz) unsalted butter
2 apples peeled and cut into thin wedges
1 tbsp honey
2 tbsp balsamic vinegar
375g (13oz) puff-pastry
150g (5oz) Camembert, sliced
Rocket leaves to garnish
For the walnut drizzle:
50g (2oz) walnuts
3-4 tbsp olive oil
1 tbsp chopped tarragon

1 Preheat the oven to 200°C/400°F/Gas Mark 6. Fry the apples. Stir in the honey and balsamic vinegar. Leave to cool.

2 Roll out the pastry to 2mm thick. Using a 6cm (2½in) cutter, stamp 12 discs. Grease 6 boat-shaped mini tart tins, 12x5cm (4x2in), and line with pastry discs. Line with baking parchment and fill with baking beans or rice.

3 Bake for 10 mins, then remove beans. Bake for a further 2-3 mins until golden. Leave to cool. Repeat with the remaining 6 discs.

4 Blitz the walnuts, oil, tarragon and salt and pepper until it looks like a lumpy pesto.

5 Fill the tart cases with the apple mixture and top each with a slice of Camembert. Bake for 8 mins until the cheese is melted. Drizzle the oil over the tarts.

Afternoon Tea by Eric Lanlard, Octopus Books, £20

8 SUNDAY

9 MONDAY

10 TUESDAY

11 WEDNESDAY

12 THURSDAY

13 FRIDAY

14 SATURDAY

Blast from the past

Dad's first car

I have wonderful memories of my dad. He was a very strong, wise, kind man. He taught me a lot which helps me even today at the age of 75.

In the 1950s nobody in our street had a car so we were delighted to hear that Dad had bought one. It was a Riley, dark green with metal wheels, registration ANX 403. We were all dying to go for a ride in it, but Dad said he had to teach himself to drive first.

Then one day he announced that he could drive and off we went! Dad took us out on his days off work. We went for picnics in nice country places as well as to Devon and Cornwall and up to St Helen's in Lancashire where my granddad, auntie, uncle and cousins lived. We even took the car ferry over the River Severn to Wales to visit my mum's family.

What a treat! It was exhilarating the way the engine roared as we drove up the hills. And I would never have seen all those lovely places if my capable dad hadn't taught himself to drive. I do miss him!

Diane Clarke, Bristol

No 1 this week

1974 Charles Aznavour: She
Known in the UK as the theme song for the TV series The Seven Faces of Women, She was written by Herbert Kretzmer, the lyricist of Les Misérables, and Charles Aznavour wrote the music. Originally the TV producer wanted the track sung by Marlene Dietrich as she represented 'the ageless woman' but Herbert Kretzmer insisted it needed to be sung by a man, and who better than Aznavour himself? As well as English Aznavour also recorded the song in Spanish, German, Italian and his native French.

What a good idea

Keep your perfume smelling fragrant all day long with the help of some handy cotton buds. Simply spray your favourite perfume on to a handful of cotton buds and put these in a plastic bag in your handbag. Then whenever you want a top-up of your scent, just reach for a cotton bud and dab on to your pulse points. Easy!

Bizarre Britain

It's sink or swim in Castletown, Isle of Man, for the World Tin Bath Championships. Run - intriguingly - by the Castletown Ale Drinkers' Society, the championships involve competitors from around the world taking to decorated tin baths. The winner is either the first across the finish line or the one who covers the furthest distance before sinking.

Portrait of a star

BING CROSBY

BORN: **May 3, 1903**
DIED: **October 14, 1977**
KNOWN FOR: **White Christmas, Holiday Inn, Going My Way, High Society**
HE SAID: **"I think popular music in this country is one of the few things in the 20th century that have made great strides in reverse."**

Recipe of the week

STRAWBERRY SALAD

Serves: 4 Preparation time: 15 mins Cooking time: 3 mins

130g (4½oz) walnuts
1 tbsp olive oil
200g (7oz) torn spinach leaves
400g (1lb) sliced strawberries
150g (5oz) soft goat's cheese
Juice of 1 lime
1 tsp dried parsley
100ml (3½oz) olive oil
Salt and black pepper

1 Sauté the walnuts in a little olive oil in a large frying pan or wok until slightly charred, cool, then chop roughly.
2 Put the spinach leaves, walnuts and sliced strawberries into a large bowl. Gently break the goat's cheese and sprinkle over the salad.
3 For the dressing, whisk the lime juice, parsley and olive oil together. Season with salt and black pepper, pour over salad, gently toss and serve.
Aldi

15 SUNDAY

16 MONDAY

17 TUESDAY

18 WEDNESDAY

19 THURSDAY

20 FRIDAY

21 SATURDAY

Blast from the past

Starting at the bottom

On leaving school in July 1952, I commenced work at Chamberlain and Arnolds, a grocery shop in Ross-on-Wye. Day one was not quite what I had expected as I'd had visions of myself in a crisp white overall standing behind a shiny counter. Instead I was introduced to Rosie who provided me with an old blue overall, a dishcloth and duster and a bucket of warm water.

We descended a flight of stairs and I found myself in a dimly-lit storeroom where I was told: "Now, I want you to wash every tin and bottle and dust every packet until you have finished." Some time later, a voice called down: "Tea is ready, Miss Owen, come for your break."

The staffroom was part of the manager's office and we sat on wooden banana boxes for our ten-minute break. We had another equally brief break in the afternoon and paid Rosie sixpence a week for our tea.

When I told my mother what I had been doing on my first day at work, she replied: "Well, you have to start at the bottom and work your way up." I did not see the funny side of that at the time!

Joan Fishbourne, Hereford

No 1 this week

1962 Frank Ifield: I Remember You
The song was one of several introduced in the 1942 film The Fleet's In and sung by Dorothy Lamour. Johnny Mercer (who co-wrote the songs with the film's director Victor Schertzinger), says he originally created I Remember You to express his infatuation for Judy Garland. Twenty years later Frank Ifield recorded the song in a yodelling country-music style and his version went on to sell more than one million copies in the UK alone - staying at No.1 for seven weeks.

What a good idea

That pack of ice cubes you've been saving in the fridge for hot days could just come in handy if you happen to have a spillage. Rub an ice cube over the spot where you've spilt something immediately and the ice will stop the stain from setting, making it easier for you to wash it away later.

Bizarre Britain

I say, my dear, have you heard of the Chap Olympiad? Monocles and sock suspenders at the ready, for it's an annual event hosted by Chap magazine for the dandies, gentleman and those whose tastes hark back to centuries past. Events at the Bloomsbury Square gathering, which has been running since 1999, include moustache-wrestling, cucumber sandwiches, discus and umbrella jousting.

Portrait of a star

MARLON BRANDO

BORN: **April 3, 1924**
DIED: **July 1, 2004**
KNOWN FOR: **The Godfather, On the Waterfront, A Streetcar Named Desire**
HE SAID: **"Never confuse the size of your pay cheque with the size of your talent."**

Recipe of the week

CHICKEN LETTUCE CUPS

Makes: 15 Preparation time: 10 mins Cooking time: 10 mins

2 tsp nut oil
8 spring onions, 6 finely sliced, 2 reserved for decoration
1-2tsp curry powder
2 tbsp crunchy peanut butter
200g (7oz) cooked chicken, torn into bite-sized pieces
80g (2¾oz) baby corn cut into ½ cm rounds
160ml (¼pt) chicken stock
50g (1½oz) creamed coconut
2 tsp soy sauce
200g (7oz) cooked brown rice
2 baby gem lettuce
Small bunch of coriander
1 lime cut in wedges

1 Heat the oil and gently cook the sliced spring onions for 2 mins. Add the curry powder and peanut butter, cook stirring for 1 min until fragrant then add the chicken and baby corn. Stir to coat.

2 Pour in the stock, coconut milk and soy, stir and cook for 10 mins. If the satay becomes too thick add a little more stock.

3 While the satay is cooking, slice the two remaining spring onions then tear the leaves from the lettuce and arrange on a serving plate. When the satay is ready, spoon a little cooked rice into each lettuce leaf then top with satay, scatter with the spring onions, coriander leaves and squeeze over a few wedges of lime.
www.makemoreofsalad.com

22 SUNDAY

23 MONDAY

24 TUESDAY

25 WEDNESDAY

26 THURSDAY

27 FRIDAY

28 SATURDAY

Blast from the past

Achtung, frauleins!

In 1946, my friend Audrey and I went as exchange students to study at a German university. The aim was to improve our spoken German. We were astonished at the devastation the war had inflicted on the quiet little town. Very few shops were left standing and it was common to see a shop window with just one item on display and very little stock available inside.

On one trip to the town centre we spotted a shop with a big notice in the window, 'Neu Angestrichen'. We knew that the word neu meant new so we thought that at last we had found a shop with some fresh stock. We dashed across the road, full of anticipation, only to find the usual empty shop window. I said: "The goods must be inside." We leaned close to the window with our hands on the sill, peering this way and that, but we could see nothing.

A few moments later we added another word to our German vocabulary when we found ourselves covered in bright yellow paint. Too late, we realised that the phrase 'neu angestrichen' meant wet paint!

The photo is of Audrey and me in the ruins of Münster; I am on the left.
Dorothy Parry, Southport

No 1 this week

1955 Slim Whitman: Rose Marie
Originally the title song of a 1924 musical, set in the Canadian Rockies and telling the story of Rose-Marie La Flemme, a French-Canadian girl who loved miner Jim Kenyon. The 1936 film adaptation featured Nelson Eddy and Jeanette McDonald, but country artist Slim Whitman made it a hit spending 11 consecutive weeks at No.1 in the UK charts, a record until 1991 when Bryan Adams' (Everything I Do) I Do It for You, spent 16 weeks at the top.

What a good idea

Packing for your holidays? Be a clever packer by putting heavier items like your shoes near the wheels of your suitcase and lighter items near the handle. This way things are less likely to get jumbled up by the time you reach your destination and items are less likely to be damaged.

Bizarre Britain

Her Majesty's mute swans are a protected species and a tradition at this time of year called Swan Upping plays a vital role in conserving them for posterity. The Royal Swan Uppers, who wear the scarlet uniform of Her Majesty the Queen, ceremoniously travel in rowing skiffs down the river to collect information on the health of young cygnets.

Portrait of a star

SOPHIA LOREN

BORN: **September 20, 1934**
KNOWN FOR: **Two Women, El Cid, Houseboat, Yesterday, Today and Tomorrow**
SHE SAID: **"Sex appeal is 50% what you've got and 50% what people think you've got."**

Recipe of the week

CLASSIC BLUEBERRY PANCAKES

Serves: 4 Preparation time: 10 mins Cooking time: 4 mins

Aunt Bessie's Pancake Mix
125g (4½oz) blueberries
250g (9oz) maple flavour syrup
½ tbsp sugar
1 medium egg
250ml (½pt) of cold water

1 Place half a pack of blueberries in a pan and add half a tbsp of sugar. Heat until blueberries are soft and sugar has dissolved.

2 To make the pancakes, add one medium egg and 250ml of cold water then whisk until smooth, then transfer the mixture to a jug.

3 Lightly oil a medium non-stick frying pan and heat until very hot. Pour in enough batter to thinly coat the base of the pan.

4 Cook for 1-2 mins on a medium heat until golden brown on the underside. Turn over then cook for a further 1-2 mins.

5 Place pancakes on a plate and spoon over the blueberries and drizzle with maple syrup. Add a spoonful of sour cream if desired.

Recipe from Iceland

29 SUNDAY

30 MONDAY

31 TUESDAY

1 WEDNESDAY

2 THURSDAY

3 FRIDAY

4 SATURDAY

Blast from the past

Saucy seagull

My family used to spend our summer holiday in Bournemouth for two weeks. My parents had friends who lived there and as they went to camp with a youth club, they let us use their house while they were away.

I loved Bournemouth with its lovely sandy beaches and a good bus service to the nearby resorts of Shell Bay, Swanage and Sandbanks (before it became known as Millionaires' Row). There was also a pretty park that was illuminated at night.

One year, my aunt, uncle and cousin Christine came with us and, armed with buckets and nets, we went for a walk to the rock pools on the beach. The tide was out so my dad rolled up his trousers and went for a paddle. His legs were lily white as they never normally saw the light of day.

Just then a seagull flew over and dropped something at his feet. It was a sandwich in a paper bag. How we laughed! My aunt teased my father, saying: "Your legs frightened that poor seagull so much it dropped its dinner!"

Such happy days when the sun seemed always to shine and simple pleasures brought much happiness.

Pamela Bish, East Grinstead

No 1 this week

1970 Elvis Presley: The Wonder of You
Elvis Presley recorded a live version of The Wonder of You in Las Vegas, Nevada in February 1970. The song was released as a single in April the same year, with Mama Liked the Roses as the B-side. The Wonder of You became one of Elvis' most successful records in the UK, topping the UK singles chart for six weeks in the summer of 1970. Over the years the song was also recorded by Ray Peterson, Ronnie Hilton, The Platters and Nelson Riddle.

What a good idea

After a long day out in summer weather, shoes can get a bit whiffy. To freshen them up, try filling an old sock with clean cat litter, tying up the end and putting into your shoe overnight. The following morning you should find the smell has gone. A sheet of fabric softener will also do the trick.

Bizarre Britain

If you see a chicken sprinting across the Derbysire town of Bonsall this August don't be alarmed. It's probably a prizewinning hen practising for the annual World Hen Racing Championships which has been going on for more than 100 years. Here hens race down 15-metre tracks, cheered on by the sound of their owners banging tins.

Portrait of a star

AUDREY HEPBURN

BORN: **May 4, 1929**
DIED: **January 20, 1993**
KNOWN FOR: **Breakfast at Tiffany's, My Fair Lady, Roman Holiday, Funny Face**
SHE SAID: **"Nothing is impossible, the word itself says 'I'm possible'!"**

Recipe of the week

BERRY AND GINGER ICE CREAM

Serves: 4 Preparation time: 5 mins

300g (11oz) mixed frozen berries
300g (11oz) of Alpro vanilla yogurt
70g (2½oz) stem ginger
1 tbsp of honey

1 Place all the ingredients in a blender or a food processer. Blend the mixture until smooth.

2 If you find the mixture isn't breaking down, leave the berries to defrost for 10 mins before blending again.

3 You want the mixture to come together easily but not turn into a sauce. Once everything has come together, scoop into bowls and serve immediately.

4 If you want to make this now and serve later, add it to a plastic Tupperware box, smooth out and keep in the freezer for a day or two. Leave to defrost for 5 mins before serving using an ice cream scoop. Add chunks of dark chocolate for a luxurious touch.
www.alpro.co.uk

5 SUNDAY

6 MONDAY

7 TUESDAY

8 WEDNESDAY

9 THURSDAY

10 FRIDAY

11 SATURDAY

Blast from the past

Mine's a cornet!

This picture still makes me smile. It was taken way back in 1958 when I was three years old. My parents used to take me and my two sisters to Woolacombe in Devon for our summer holidays every year.

On this particular day I was allowed to go to the ice-cream van for a cornet all on my own. It was quite a long way for a little girl and in my haste I dropped it on the way back. I was inconsolable! My parents gave me another threepenny bit to go again, but this time I was instructed to bring the cornet and the wrapped ice cream back to them for assembly.

I've always loved the photo my dad took of me returning, earnestly clutching both items and no doubt very worried that my precious ice cream might start melting at any moment. See how I am kicking up the sand in my rush to get back to our picnic area.

These days, I only wear such an intensely focused expression when I am heading for the bar!

Dianne Copeland, by email

No 1 this week

1959 Cliff Richard & The Drifters: Living Doll
Featured on the soundtrack to Cliff's debut film, Serious Charge, Living Doll was written by Lionel Bart who also wrote the West End and Broadway musical Oliver. Cliff and his backing band thought that the song was uncool, they originally weren't planning to record it but Bruce Welch, suggested a slower tempo would work better, so they rearranged it into the now familiar pace. In 1986 Cliff did a humorous, anarchic re-recording of this song for Comic Relief featuring the cast of BBC's comedy Young Ones.

What a good idea

As we hit peak ice lolly season, avoid the sticky fingers of your grandchildren by slotting a spare paper cake case on to the end of the ice lolly stick. This way, all the drips from the lolly should collect in the paper case which you can throw away, making it altogether less messy.

Bizarre Britain

You'll need your wellies in Palnackie in Scotland for the World Flounder Tramping Competition where competitors wade through mud looking for fish lying on the river bed called flounders. All catches are today kept in water to keep them alive, but it's a great excuse for a lot of mud-wrestling and muck slinging.

Portrait of a star

RITA HAYWORTH

BORN: **October 17, 1918**
DIED: **May 14, 1987**
KNOWN FOR: **Gilda, Cover Girl, The Lady From Shanghai, Blood and Sand**
SHE SAID: **"After all, a girl is... well, a girl. It's nice to be told you're successful at it."**

Recipe of the week

CHICKEN AND KALE SALAD

Serves: 2 Preparation time: 15 mins

1 tsp peanut or coconut oil
1 shallot, finely sliced
1 lemongrass stalk, bruised
1 clove garlic, crushed
¼ tsp chilli powder
¼ tsp turmeric
¼ tsp ground ginger
4 tbsp natural yogurt
1 cooked chicken breast, shredded
½ pomegranate
1x bag of baby kale
Small bunch coriander
Squeeze of lemon juice, to serve

1 Gently cook the shallot and lemongrass in a little oil until softened. Add the garlic, spices and a pinch of salt and cook for a further few minutes. Take off the heat and stir in the yogurt to create a creamy spiced mixture.

2 Mix together the shredded chicken, yogurt and pomegranate seeds. This can be cooled and refrigerated until needed.

3 Just before you're ready to eat, stir through the kale and a few torn sprigs of coriander. Add a squeeze of lemon and serve.

Discover kale

12 SUNDAY

13 MONDAY

14 TUESDAY

15 WEDNESDAY

16 THURSDAY

17 FRIDAY

18 SATURDAY

Blast from the past

Good old Skeggy!

I wonder if anyone else remembers the Derbyshire Miners' holiday camp at Skegness? It was called the poor man's Butlin's in the Fifties. My dad was a miner all his working life and we lived in the village of Carr Vale near Bolsover. The miners used to pay a set amount out of their wages which was subsidised by the local Coal Board so that they and their families could have a holiday every year.

We had great fun in Skegness and made new friends every year. My last holiday there was in 1958 when I was 17 years old. Rock 'n' roll was at its height so we teenagers had lots of happy nights dancing. I met an amazing lad called Barry and we dated for a while, but as we came from different villages and didn't have cars back then we drifted apart.

Eventually, we both got married to different people, but I never forgot him and the other friends in our crowd, Tanya, Chuck and Dawn. The photo is of me and Dawn (I am on the left). If they are still around I would love to hear from them.

Glenice Reelihaugh, Northants

No 1 this week

1982 Dexy's Midnight Runners: Come On Eileen
Based on a true story about Dexy's singer Kevin Rowland and a girl called Eileen that he grew up with, Come On Eileen, with its banjo, accordion and fiddle sounded completely different to the synthesiser pop that was popular at the time. It was the biggest-selling single of the year in the UK and much of the success was attributed to the video - which was played almost constantly on MTV at the time.

What a good idea

Ironing can be a chore at any time of year but especially so in summer when it's hot and you'd rather be enjoying the garden. Speed up the whole thing by popping a sheet of aluminium foil underneath your ironing board cover. The foil bounces the heat back up into the fabric helping make lighter work of your laundry.

Bizarre Britain

Hold your noses for the Isle of Wight Garlic Festival. Every August, the rolling green hills and farmland of Newchurch are filled with the whiff of garlic as dozens of garlic stalls, marquees and demonstrations come to town. Here you'll also find Britain's most pungent garlic as well as garlic fudge, garlic scones and even garlic ice cream!

Portrait of a star

SEAN CONNERY

BORN: **August 25, 1930**

KNOWN FOR: **Dr No, The Hunt For Red October, From Russia With Love, Goldfinger**

HE SAID: **"I like women. I don't understand them, but I like them."**

Recipe of the week

BLUEBERRY CUPCAKES

Serves: 12 Preparation time: 15 mins Cooking time: 20 mins

115g (4oz) butter or margarine
15g (½oz) granulated Stevia
2 medium eggs
140g (5oz) self-raising flour
125g (4½oz) blueberries
For the icing:
75g (3oz) butter or margarine
75g (3oz) icing sugar
125g (4½oz) low-fat cream cheese
125g (4½oz) blueberries
50g (2oz) halved raspberries

1. Preheat the oven to 200°C/400°F/Gas Mark 6. Place 12 muffin cases in a muffin tray.
2. Beat the butter or margarine with granulated Stevia until light and fluffy. Then gradually beat in the eggs before folding in the flour and blueberries.
3. Divide the batter between the cases. Bake for 20 mins, then cool on a wire rack.
4. Meanwhile, beat the butter or margarine and icing sugar until smooth.
5. Stir in the low-fat cream cheese. Spread the icing on top of the cupcakes and arrange the blueberries and halved raspberries to make flowers on each cake.

www.bakewithstork.com

19 SUNDAY

20 MONDAY

21 TUESDAY

22 WEDNESDAY

23 THURSDAY

24 FRIDAY

25 SATURDAY

Blast from the past

A case of confetti

On a sunny day in August 1960 we drove to our church wedding in a car lent by a friend. The old pub nearby supplied the wedding breakfast of boiled ham and we had a lovely three-tier cake topped with flowers.

We had to leave before the end of the meal to catch the train to Scarborough for our honeymoon. My granny gave us a cheque for £17 to cover the cost of the hotel and travel, with a little spending money for the week.

When we arrived in Scarborough and opened our suitcase we found it was full of confetti. It needed to be carefully emptied to remove all embarrassing traces of our wedding day. We were very young and felt conspicuous among all the older residents. But our secret was out – on the last day, I found a tiny silver horseshoe on my side plate at breakfast. We looked sheepishly around the dining room while everyone clapped!

The sea mist and chilly east wind drove us indoors to play bingo instead of going to the beach. This proved very lucrative and fruit dishes, knives and forks and bedspreads all went into the suitcase to help furnish our little house.
Pauline O'Daly, Saddleworth

No 1 this week

**1974 Three Degrees:
When Will I See You Again?**
Written by the Philadelphia songwriting partnership of Kenny Gamble and Leon Huff; when lead singer Sheila Ferguson first heard When Will I See You Again? she hated the song because she thought it was too ridiculously simple and vowed she would never sing it. She did of course and several million copies later realised she was wrong. The Three Degrees performed the song at Prince Charles' 30th birthday party at Buckingham Palace in 1978.

What a good idea

As you pack your suitcase for your holidays, take a moment to pop your shoes in a shower cap to stop them damaging your clothes in transit. Be sure, too, to stuff your socks into your shoes to help them keep their shape throughout the journey – which will also save on space!

Bizarre Britain

Of all the sports to combine, we wouldn't have thought of combining cycling with snorkelling. But that's just what the World Mountain Bike Bog Snorkelling in Llanwrtyd Wells, Wales is all about. Here competitors cycle along the bottom of a 6ft deep water-filled trench through the local bog wearing a lead weight belt to avoid floating away mid-pedal.

Portrait of a star

MARILYN MONROE

BORN: **June 1, 1926**
DIED: **August 5, 1962**
KNOWN FOR: **Some Like It Hot, The Seven Year Itch, Gentlemen Prefer Blondes**
SHE SAID: **"Imperfection is beauty, madness is genius and it's better to be absolutely ridiculous than absolutely boring."**

Recipe of the week

VEGETABLE BRUSCHETTA

Serves: 4 Preparation time: 10 mins Cooking time: 10 mins

1 tbsp black treacle
3 tbsp olive oil
2 tbsp lemon juice
1 garlic clove, crushed
4 thick slices of sourdough or rustic-style bread
2 large courgettes, sliced diagonally
200g (7oz) roasted peppers (from a jar), drained
Few shavings of Parmesan cheese
Freshly ground black pepper
Basil or parsley sprigs, to garnish

1 Preheat a char-grill pan or your grill. Mix together the black treacle, olive oil, lemon juice and garlic. Brush the slices of bread with this mixture, then grill the bread on both sides.
3 Brush the courgette slices with the glaze and grill for 1 min until tender. Arrange them on the bread with torn-up strips of roasted pepper.
4 Finish off with Parmesan cheese shavings, black pepper and some basil leaves or parsley sprigs. Drizzle with the remaining glaze, then serve.
Lyles

26 SUNDAY

27 MONDAY

28 TUESDAY

29 WEDNESDAY

30 THURSDAY

31 FRIDAY

1 SATURDAY

Blast from the past
Learning to teach

I was very excited when in September 1956 I took the train from Waterloo to Exmouth to take up my place as a teacher training student. My new friend Barbara and I shared a comfortable room overlooking the sea at our hall of residence, Dunsinane.

After breakfast the next day we were given a tour of the college and met the principal before being given our weekly timetable. After that we went to Exmouth to buy the stationery we would need.

I spent my first half-term holiday in Torquay (where this photo was taken at Kent's Cavern). When my relatives from Torquay came to visit me we had lunch at the Deer Leap pub. On Sundays, a group of students from Dunsinane used to walk to Littleham Church for worship.

The following September I had to have an operation on my foot. My course work arrived by post until I was able to return to college in November. I was busy and time passed very quickly until July 1958 when I qualified as a teacher and took up a post teaching religious studies and other subjects at Matthew Arnold school in Staines.

Priscilla Odell, Middlesex

No 1 this week

1976 Elton John & Kiki Dee: Don't Go Breaking My Heart

Don't Go Breaking My Heart was born out of Kiki Dee and Elton John's love of Motown duets by the likes of Marvin Gaye and Tammi Terrell and they decided to record their own. Elton and his songwriting partner Bernie Taupin wrote this song under the pseudonyms Ann Orson and Carte Blanche. Elton recorded his part in Toronto and sent the tape to London where Kiki Dee recorded her vocal. It was Elton's first UK No.1 hit and he had to wait 14 years for his next one.

What a good idea

Give your showerhead a deep clean with the help of some key kitchen cupboard ingredients. After having a shower, fill a sandwich bag with baking soda and vinegar and tie it around the showerhead, securing with an elastic band. Leave this overnight to soak and then remove in the morning. Clean off any debris with an old toothbrush.

Bizarre Britain

We know you can't beat a good dousing of gravy on a roast dinner, but how about wrestling in the stuff? That's just what they do for the World Gravy Championship in Lancashire where wrestlers in fancy dress grapple with each other in 1,000 litres of gravy. The loser then gets gravy bombed in the laughing stocks.

Portrait of a star

FRANK SINATRA

BORN: **December 12, 1915**
DIED: **May 14, 1998**
KNOWN FOR: **From Here To Eternity, The Manchurian Candidate, Ocean's 11, High Society**
HE SAID: **"You better get busy living, because dying's a pain in the ass."**

Recipe of the week

CORN FRITTERS

Serves: 4 Preparation time: 15 mins Cooking time: 30 mins

60g (2½oz) plain flour
90g (3oz) cornflour
¼ tsp baking powder
½ tsp salt
1 tsp ground cumin
1 egg
125ml (4¼oz) milk/Alpro almond milk
350g (12oz) sweetcorn kernels
16 baby plum tomatoes, halved
2 cloves garlic, crushed
1 tbsp chopped fresh thyme
Olive oil
Salt and pepper
1 tbsp balsamic vinegar
2 handfuls of baby spinach leaves
Sunflower oil

1 Preheat the oven to 200ºC/400°F/Gas Mark 6. Sift the dry ingredients into a bowl. In a separate bowl, mix the egg with the milk and then add this mixture to the dry ingredients and whisk until smooth. Add the sweetcorn and mix to combine.

2 Place the tomatoes on a baking tray and sprinkle over the crushed garlic, thyme, salt and pepper and a little olive oil. Bake for 20-30 mins until tender. Remove from the oven and sprinkle with the balsamic vinegar.

3 Heat a little sunflower oil in a non-stick frying pan until hot, spoon in the batter a tbsp at a time and cook the fritters on both sides. They should take about 5 mins on both sides, or until firm and golden brown.

4 Place a couple of the fritters on a plate and top with the tomatoes and the spinach to serve.
Alpro

2 SUNDAY

3 MONDAY

4 TUESDAY

5 WEDNESDAY

6 THURSDAY

7 FRIDAY

8 SATURDAY

Blast from the past

So unfair!

When I was at school I loved all sport, but my dearest love was netball. My friends and I had been practising in our dinner hour before a match that was coming up on the Saturday. It was very warm and we were thirsty so when we had finished playing, someone suggested we should go and get our bottles of milk which our teacher had, for some reason, forgotten to give out during the morning break. (This was when schoolchildren received a free bottle of milk every day.)

We trooped though the garden to our newly-built classroom which was some way apart from the rest of the school buildings. When we got there, we found the door was locked so it was suggested that one of us should climb in through the window. As I was the smallest, I was elected. In I went, but as I was passing out the milk bottles, the teacher came in through the door. I was sent to the head who gave me three whacks on my hand with the cane. Oh, it did sting! And the unfair thing was that the others got away scot-free!

In the photo, I am second from left in the front row.

Joyce Clifford, Ledbury

No 1 this week

1982 Survivor: Eye of The Tiger
Most memorable as the theme song for the film Rocky III, Eye of The Tiger was the biggest hit for rock band Survivor. The film's star, writer and director Sylvester Stallone asked Survivor to write the track after Queen denied permission to use their song Another One Bites the Dust. The song was nominated for an Oscar but lost out to Up Where We Belong from An Officer and a Gentleman.

What a good idea

If you need to cut a cake horizontally to make two layers, try marking where you'd like to cut your layer with tooth picks slotted in at regular intervals around the cake sides. Then wrap a length of dental floss around the cake, resting on the tooth picks, cross the two ends of the floss and pull.

Bizarre Britain

Is it a bird? Is it a plane? No it's a human-powered flying machine. Every year the seaside town of Bognor Regis plays host to the International Bognor Birdman, where people chuck themselves off the pier and take to the skies in a variety of human flying contraptions, sometimes while in fancy dress, to fundraise for charities.

Portrait of a star

REX HARRISON

BORN: **March 5, 1908**
DIED: **June 2, 1990**
KNOWN FOR: **My Fair Lady, Doctor Dolittle, The Ghost and Mrs Muir, Cleopatra**
HE SAID: **"Exhilaration is that feeling you get just after a great idea hits you, and just before you realise what's wrong with it."**

Recipe of the week

SPICED BLACK FOREST CRUMBLE

Serves: 4-6 Preparation time: 15 mins
Cooking time: 25-30 mins

450g (1lb) bag of frozen black forest fruits
Zest and juice of 1 orange
1 tsp honey
1 tsp cinnamon
50g (2oz) low-fat spread
125g (4½oz) spelt flour
40g (1½oz) caster sugar
40g (1½oz) fruit and nut muesli

1 Preheat the oven to 190ºC/375ºF/Gas Mark 5. Tip the defrosted frozen black forest fruits with any juices into individual pudding bowls or a 1 litre (1¾pt) baking dish.
2 Whisk the zest and juice of the orange, honey and cinnamon together and pour over the fruit. In a bowl, rub the spread into the flour to form fine breadcrumbs. Stir in the sugar and muesli and scatter the mixture over the fruit. Bake for 25-30 mins, until the top is golden and crisp.
www.waitrose.com/recipes

9 SUNDAY

10 MONDAY

11 TUESDAY

12 WEDNESDAY

13 THURSDAY

14 FRIDAY

15 SATURDAY

Blast from the past

A return visit

I was only six when I was evacuated. I was taken to a London train station and travelled nearly all day. We were taken to a village hall to sleep overnight. The next day we continued our journey until we reached the lovely village of Cartmel in the Lake District.

I was chosen by a Mrs Chambers, a widow who had a son, Harry. They lived in a cottage called Fell View, a short distance from the village school which had only two classrooms. Mrs Chambers was a district nurse. She was very kind, but quite strict. The only thing I didn't like about living there was the outside toilet.

This photo was taken over fifty years later when my husband and I visited Cartmel and found it was exactly as I remembered. We walked through the village and found the cottage. There was an elderly gentleman in the garden. When my husband explained why we were there, he ushered us inside to meet his wife whose parents used to rent the cottage to Mrs Chambers. We had tea and cakes and I was invited to look round the cottage which had hardly changed and brought back memories of long ago.

Jean Carter, York

No 1 this week

1963 The Beatles: She Loves You
In the UK She Loves You was The Beatles biggest-selling single, it also held the record for the top-selling UK single of all time until 1977, when Wings (led by Paul McCartney) topped it with Mull of Kintyre. Lennon and McCartney wrote the track on June 26, 1963 after a concert at the Majestic Ballroom with Roy Orbison and Gerry and the Pacemakers. McCartney was inspired by the 'call and response' style of Bobby Rydell's hit Forget Him.

What a good idea

Garden tools might not look their best after a busy summer but you can easily revive them ready for next year. Mix together play sand and baby oil in a small bucket or pot until just dampened. Then pull your tools in and out of the sand mixture. The abrasive sand will sharpen while the baby oil will stop rust.

Bizarre Britain

Yorkshire and Lancashire have long held a grudge against each other but in Ramsbottom, Lancashire, they like to settle the score with an annual battle of the puddings. For the World Black Pudding Throwing Championship, Lancastrians hurl black puddings at a 20-foot high plinth stacked with a pile of Yorkshire puddings.

Portrait of a star

CAROLE LOMBARD

BORN: **October 6, 1908**
DIED: **January 16, 1942**
KNOWN FOR: **My Man Godfrey, Nothing Sacred, Mr & Mrs Smith, To Be Or Not To Be**
SHE SAID: **"A woman has just as much right in this world as a man and can get along in it just as well if she puts her mind to it."**

Recipe of the week

BLACKBERRY CHIA AND LEMON PUDDING

Serves: 4 Preparation time: 25 mins
Cooking time: 35-40 mins

1 tbsp oil
Zest of 1 lemon
100g (4oz) caster sugar
100g (4oz) margarine
2 eggs
100g (4oz) self-raising flour
4 tsp chia seeds
150g (5oz) blackberries
For the custard:
1 tbsp cornflour
2 egg yolks
Juice of 1 lemon
100g puréed blackberries

1 Preheat oven to 180°C/350°F/Gas Mark 4. Brush 4, 200ml (7fl oz) metal pudding moulds with oil then line bases with a circle of baking paper.
2 Blitz the lemon zest with the sugar in a food processor.
3 Add the margarine and blitz until smooth. Add the eggs and flour and mix until smooth.
4 Stir in the chia seeds and blackberries. Divide between pudding moulds. Cover each with a square of oiled foil then stand them in a roasting tin that is half filled with boiling water.
5 Cover tin with foil and bake for 35-40 mins. Make the custard by mixing the cornflour with 2 tbsp water in a pan.
6 Mix in the egg yolks and when smooth, stir in the lemon juice and puréed blackberries. Bring to boil and stir until thick.
7 Remove from heat and stir until smooth. Drizzle over cooked puds.
www.seasonalberries.co.uk

16 SUNDAY

17 MONDAY

18 TUESDAY

19 WEDNESDAY

20 THURSDAY

21 FRIDAY

22 SATURDAY

Blast from the past

A lesson learned

When I was a little girl, before the days of 'health and safety', I lived in an old house that had been temporarily divided up into four flats. I lived in a top flat with my mum and dad and younger brother. My friend lived in the flat underneath with her mum, dad and brother.

Our kitchen was just a converted bathroom. One day my mother caught the chip pan alight by accident and we all started screaming. I am not sure if our neighbour downstairs heard us or whether we ran down to get her, but she came up and threw a jug of water over the pan. The fat went everywhere and my mum got her legs burned - not badly enough to go to the doctor, luckily. It taught us all the lesson never to throw water over a chip pan.

Another time, when I was fighting with my brother, we knocked over one of those round enamel stoves with a handle on top (we had no central heating in the flat). As quick as a flash, my mum picked the stove up by the handle and put it upright before it burst into flames.

Jean Walker, Thatcham

No 1 this week

1968 The Beatles: Hey Jude
Paul McCartney originally wrote this as Hey Jules, because the song was meant to comfort John Lennon's five-year-old son Julian as his parents were getting a divorce. The change to 'Jude' was apparently inspired by the character Jud in the musical Oklahoma! At more than seven minutes long it was the longest song ever released as a single at the time, it was also the first to be released on The Beatles' own record label, Apple Records.

What a good idea

If grandchildren have got a little creative with their drawing skills and left crayon marks over your walls, you can easily remove them with the help of a hairdryer. Just heat the hairdryer over the surface to melt the crayon and then wipe away with washing-up liquid on a damp cloth.

Bizarre Britain

For centuries, gurning competitions have existed, encouraging us to pull the funniest faces we can. But one place where this still survives today is Egremont, West Cumbria, where the World Gurning Championships is held as part of the annual Crab Fair, which dates back to 1267. Here 'gurners' must pull grotesque faces through a horse collar, known as a braffin.

Portrait of a star

KATHARINE HEPBURN

BORN: **May 12, 1907**
DIED: **June 29, 2003**
KNOWN FOR: **On Golden Pond, The African Queen, The Philadelphia Story**
SHE SAID: **"Love has nothing to do with what you are expecting to get - only with what you are expecting to give - which is everything."**

Recipe of the week

POACHED PEARS WITH CHOCOLATE SAUCE AND PISTACHIOS

Serves: 2 Preparation time: 10 mins Cooking time: 30 mins

25g (1oz) caster sugar
1 cinnamon stick
2 small peeled pears
40g (1½oz) plain chocolate
50ml (2 floz) evaporated milk
15g (½oz) roughly chopped pistachio nuts

1 Place the sugar, cinnamon stick and 300ml (10fl oz) water in a small pan and gently heat to dissolve the sugar.
2 Add the pears, cover and simmer over a low heat for 20-30 mins or until the pears are soft.
3 To make the chocolate sauce, melt the chocolate in a small heatproof bowl over a pan of boiling water. Once the chocolate has melted stir in the evaporated milk.
4 Remove the pears from the sugar solution, slice in half and transfer to a serving dish, drizzle over the chocolate sauce and sprinkle over the pistachio nuts.
www.americanpistachios.co.uk

23 SUNDAY

24 MONDAY

25 TUESDAY

26 WEDNESDAY

27 THURSDAY

28 FRIDAY

29 SATURDAY

Blast from the past

A shipboard romance

In the summer of 1959 I was just 17 and working as a nanny for a family in Essex. When we had a day off my friend Eileen and I took a day trip from Clacton-on-Sea to Calais on The Queen of the Channel. On the way across the assistant purser came over to chat to us. I thought he looked very handsome in his uniform.

Eileen and I had a great time in Calais and I still have the necklace I bought. The return journey took longer as the sea was rough. The assistant purser invited me into his office and asked me to write my address on a small brown envelope. Later, I received a letter in this envelope asking me to meet him in Colchester on my 18th birthday. Soon after that, he joined the New Zealand Shipping Company and was away for three months. He wrote long letters from every port which I have kept to this day.

When he returned he proposed to me on Liverpool Street underground station. I accepted and we were married in September 1962. It was all very romantic! Now we have three sons and seven grandchildren.
Hazel Moysey, Kingston-upon-Thames

No 1 this week

1965 Ken Dodd: Tears
Tears was the biggest UK hit in 1965, selling 1,521,000 copies, but not everyone loved it. Ken Dodd later recalled: "The disc-jockeys hated it - they couldn't find words that were bad enough to say about it, but it didn't matter. The public was ready for a tuneful, singalong song and you can't keep a good song down. You can be the squarest of squares, but if you make a good record, you can still get there."

What a good idea

Breaking in a new pair of shoes? Prevent blisters on your heels and toes by giving your new shoes a quick spritz of deodorant on the inside where they might rub. This should stop the friction that makes our feet hurt. As an added bonus, your feet will smell amazing too!

Bizarre Britain

As children, we may have learned the joy of skimming stones, but on Easdale Island, the smallest permanently inhabited island in the Inner Hebrides, they take this to a whole new level with the Stone Skimming Championship. Started as a fundraiser in 1983, contestants send stones skimming over the water and the one which goes the furthest distance wins.

Portrait of a star

ROCK HUDSON

BORN: **November 17, 1925**
DIED: **October 2, 1985**
KNOWN FOR: **Giant, Pillow Talk, Come September, Lover Come Back**
HE SAID: **"Someone asked me once what my philosophy of life was, and I said some crazy thing. I should have said, how the hell do I know?"**

Recipe of the week

PEAR FLAN

Serves: 6 Preparation time: 15 mins Cooking time: 40 mins

250g (9oz) tinned pears
40g (1½oz) ground almonds
10 tsp Table Top sweetener
2 medium eggs
150ml (5floz) soya milk
1½ tbsp soya single cream
½ tsp vanilla bean paste or vanilla essence
Almond flakes, to decorate
Icing sugar to decorate

1 Preheat the oven to 180°C/160°F/Gas Mark 6. Grease an ovenproof dish then slice the tinned pears and arrange them neatly in the greased dish.

2 In a bowl, whisk two eggs until aerated and add the sweetener and vanilla bean paste into the mixture. Stir in the ground almonds and mix. Pour in the soya milk and soya single cream while stirring.

3 Pour the entire mixture on top of the pears in the dish, and place in the oven for 35-40 mins, or until cooked.

4 Sprinkle the almond flakes on the flan and return to the oven for a further 15 mins. Use a skewer to check the centre of the flan, which should come out clean if cooked.

Heart UK

30 SUNDAY

1 MONDAY

2 TUESDAY

3 WEDNESDAY

4 THURSDAY

5 FRIDAY

6 SATURDAY

Blast from the past

Horse-mad sisters

This is a photo of me (on the left) with my horse, Gay, and my younger sister Bev with her pony, Domino. We used to attach those long fringes to their halters when they went out to graze in the summer to keep the flies away from their eyes. (Looking at the picture now, it strikes me that Bev and I had done very much the same thing with our own hairstyles!)

Growing up, we always had ponies and horses, but as we lived on a housing estate in Kent, we had to keep them at livery. My dad was perfectly content in this nice home with all mod-cons but he was eventually worn down by his girls (me, my sister and Mum – who was as horse-mad as we were, although she didn't ride) and agreed to move to an extremely run-down house with no heating and a leaking roof, all for the sake of having our own paddock! This photo was taken soon after we moved there.

But Dad came up trumps all round. The decrepit house eventually became a lovely, comfortable home and he single-handedly built stables, complete with a tack and feed room, for our beloved horses.
Lesley Howard, Norfolk

No 1 this week

1957 Paul Anka: Diana
Paul Anka wrote Diana when he was a love-struck 15 year old. Rumours abound about who Diana actually was; some say she was his sister's babysitter, a girl at church or a friend from high school. Whichever is true the love seems to have been unrequited. Anka was the first teenager to have a million-seller in the UK - he was still only 15 when it charted.

What a good idea

Always losing the end of your sewing thread and then struggling to get it back on the needle? You need some hairspray. Spraying the end of a thread of cotton with hairspray will make it stiff enough for you to thread it through the eye of the needle much easier. Just remember not to lick it afterwards!

Bizarre Britain

Every year Somerset plays host to a specialist sport that requires skill, strength and cunning. The event? Mangold Hurling! Mangold Wurzels are vegetables of the beet family and for one weekend every October competitors in Somerset like to hurl their Mangolds at a target called the Norman. The thrower whose Mangold lands closest to the Norman wins!

Portrait of a star

HEDY LAMARR

BORN: **November 9, 1914**
DIED: **January 19, 2000**
KNOWN FOR: **Samson and Delilah, Ecstasy, The Strange Woman, White Cargo**
SHE SAID: **"Any girl can be glamorous. All you have to do is stand still and look stupid."**

Recipe of the week

APPLE FLAPJACKS

Serves: 8 Preparation time: 10 mins Cooking time: 30 mins

1kg (2lb 3oz) apples, peeled, cored and grated
40g (1½oz) sugar
150g (5oz) butter
70ml (2½fl oz) golden syrup
200g (7oz) oats
Pinch of salt
Pinch of ground ginger

1 In a pan sprinkle the apples with the sugar, cover and cook over a gentle heat until they become soft.
2 Add the butter and golden syrup and bring to a gentle simmer.
3 Gently stir in the oats, salt and ginger. Pour the mixture into a buttered cake tin 20.5cm (8in) and bake in the oven at 180°C/350°F/Gas Mark 4 for 30 mins. Allow to cool before turning out.
Pink Lady Apples

7 SUNDAY

8 MONDAY

9 TUESDAY

10 WEDNESDAY

11 THURSDAY

12 FRIDAY

13 SATURDAY

Blast from the past

My true love

I met Derek, my first love, when we were still at school. He was 17 and I was 15. We dated for two years, then I met Peter and finished with Derek. My mother told me I was making the biggest mistake of my life, but I didn't listen.

I married Peter, but the marriage didn't last long. I married again and had four children, a boy and then triplets. When the triplets were three, I got divorced and brought my children up alone. One day, I bumped into Derek in the supermarket. He was also divorced with three children. He suggested we should have a night out for old times' sake and that was the beginning of the best part of my life.

I knew that I had always loved him as I'd kept the spinning heart he bought me for my 16th birthday. We have been together for 25 years. He is a wonderful husband and my best friend. Twelve years ago I was diagnosed with Non-Hodgkins' lymphoma for which I am still having treatment. He has been by my side all the way and calls it 'our lymphoma'. He is the love of my life.

Lynn Greaves, by email

No 1 this week

1980 **Police: Don't Stand So Close to Me**
Don't Stand So Close to Me concerns a schoolgirl's crush on her teacher and the resulting affair, which is ultimately discovered. As The Police's lead singer Sting, had been a teacher before he joined the band many people assumed the lyrics were autobiographical. In 1982 the song won the Grammy Award for Best Rock Performance by a Group or Duo.

What a good idea

Avid sewing enthusiasts may find that fabric scissors don't work as well as they used to after years of use, which can be awkward when crafting or dressmaking. To make them like new, cut through a couple of sheets of sandpaper. This should sharpen up their edges and have them snipping well again.

Bizarre Britain

Conker fights were a vital part of our autumn school days but in Southwick, Northamptonshire they like to prove it's not just for children with the annual World Conker Championships. A coin is flipped before two conker masters go head to head with their conker nuts and laces, especially provided by the Ashton Conker Club to ensure all is fair.

Portrait of a star

MAGGIE SMITH

BORN: **December 28, 1934**

KNOWN FOR: **The Prime of Miss Jean Brodie, A Room With A View, Death on the Nile,**

SHE SAID: **"There's a difference between solitude and loneliness."**

Recipe of the week

PEAR AND GINGER PUFF TART

Serves: 4 Preparation time: 25 mins
Cooking time: 20 mins

1 ready made puff-pastry block
2-3 tbsp ginger preserve
2 ripe pears
1 orange
1 beaten egg

1. Preheat oven to 220°C/425°F/Gas Mark 7. Roll out the puff pastry and cut out a 23cm (9in) disc using a sharp knife.

2. Place on a lined baking sheet and spread centre with 2-3 tbsp of the ginger preserve leaving a 2cm (½ in) border.

3. Halve and remove cores from pears then cut each half into medium-thick slices. Toss sliced pears in juice of one orange and arrange on the pastry disc - overlapping slices to form a circle.

4. Brush pastry border with 1 beaten egg and bake for 18-20 mins until pastry is risen and golden.

5. Scatter with orange rind before serving.
Recipe from Jus-Rol

14 SUNDAY

15 MONDAY

16 TUESDAY

17 WEDNESDAY

18 THURSDAY

19 FRIDAY

20 SATURDAY

Blast from the past

Saturdays were special

When I was a little girl, I used to look forward to Saturdays as they were totally different from every other day of the week. All the mothers in our street used to be out in force 'creaming' the doorsteps while we children played in a field behind the houses or a small park close by. I was usually accompanied by our dog – and both of us were strictly forbidden to stand on the clean doorstep.

When the milkman turned up, pushing two churns on his barrow, the women went out with jugs to get their milk for the weekend. The greengrocer used to call with his horse-drawn cart on which the vegetables and fruit were beautifully displayed. Fruit was considered an expensive luxury in those days so the children used to ask him if he had any bruised or damaged apples to give away.

On Saturdays, it was a tradition for my mother and eldest sister to get dressed up, put on their hats, and go shopping together in the city's department stores. My older brother would go off to play football and my father would usually be doing something useful around the house.

June Myles, Chipping Ongar

No 1 this week

1967 Bee Gees: Massachusetts
Written by Barry, Robin and Maurice Gibb, Massachusetts became the Bee Gees first of five No.1 hits in the UK. The brothers wrote the song (despite never having been to Massachusetts) intending it for The Seekers who, like the Bee Gees, had travelled to the UK from Australia. When they were unsuccessful getting the song to Judith Durham's band they decided to record it themselves. Massachusetts also reached No.1 in 12 other countries and ultimately sold more than five million copies worldwide.

What a good idea

Microwaves can easily get messy, especially if you have a dinner explosion in there! Clean your microwave the easy way by mixing two tablespoons of white vinegar and a few drops of your favourite essential oil with water and blast it for five minutes. You'll be left with a shiny clean microwave that smells great and zero scrubbing required.

Bizarre Britain

Banbury, Oxfordshire welcomes the arrival of some unusual equines and their companions as the hobby horse festival comes to town. Celebrating the ancient hobby horse of lore and legend where men dressed in wickerwork and cloth costumes designed to look like horses for May Day parades and seasonal celebrations, here Banbury comes to life with capering, neighing and Maypole dancing.

Portrait of a star

LAUREN BACALL

BORN: **September 16, 1924**
DIED: **August 12, 2014**
KNOWN FOR: **To Have and Have Not, The Big Sleep, Key Largo, Dark Passage**
SHE SAID: **"Think your whole life shows in your face and you should be proud of that."**

Recipe of the week

CRISPY CRUMB COD WITH PEAS AND MASH

Serves: 4 Preparation time: 5 mins Cooking time: 10 mins

300g (10½oz) can marrowfat peas
600g (21oz) frozen or ready-prepared mashed potato
4 150g (5oz) cod fillets
2 large tomatoes, sliced
100g (3½oz) mature cheddar cheese, grated
4 tbsp dried breadcrumbs
Salt and freshly ground black pepper
Fresh parsley, to garnish

1. Preheat the grill. Tip the can of peas into a saucepan and heat gently, stirring often.
2. Heat the mashed potato according to pack instructions.
3. Meanwhile, arrange the cod fillets on the grill rack and top them with the sliced tomatoes. Grill for 3-4 mins.
4. Mix the grated cheese and breadcrumbs together and sprinkle on top of the fish. Season. Grill for another 3-4 mins, or until the fish flakes easily.
5. Mix the peas and mashed potato together and spoon on to warm serving plates. Arrange the cod fillets on top and serve garnished with fresh parsley.

Batchelors Mushy Peas

21 SUNDAY

22 MONDAY

23 TUESDAY

24 WEDNESDAY

25 THURSDAY

26 FRIDAY

27 SATURDAY

Blast from the past

Open all hours

My sister and I were born in the 1950s. We lived in Huddersfield within walking distance of a baker, two butchers, a grocer and a newsagent. We often went to the corner shops with Mum's shopping list where we used to listen to the grown ups chatting while we waited patiently for our turn in the queue.

Our earwigging came in useful when we spent hours playing with the custom-built shop that we were given as our big present one Christmas. It had been custom-made by a local joiner and had a red Formica-topped counter with a matching shelf unit painted bright yellow. It also had a smart cash till and a small set of scales to weigh out precious dolly mixtures.

Our Great Uncle John stencilled our opening times in Indian ink while we made adverts and price cards. Our props included Mum's old purses and handbags and netted shopping bags. We stacked our shelves with a set of early Sixties mini packages with some homemade additions such as hundreds and thousands sweets.

Our local gang of friends provided us with (sometimes awkward) customers to complete our own mini version of Arkwright's store in Open All Hours.

Janice Leadbeater, by email

No 1 this week

1969 Archies: Sugar, Sugar
The Archies were a group of fictional teenagers from the Saturday morning cartoon show Archie. Don Kirshner, a prolific promoter and producer who had created The Monkees, said he wanted to do something similar but with cartoon characters because they are much easier to work with! The song Sugar, Sugar, written by Jeff Barry and Andy Kim, quickly became a No.1 hit in the US, largely thanks to the TV show, and spent eight weeks at the top of the UK charts, too.

What a good idea

To make life easier when selecting your outfit in the morning, rethink how you organise your bedroom cupboards and drawers. Try folding and stacking your clothes vertically, side by side, rather than horizontally with one on top of another. This way you can easily see all the clothes at a glance. It'll also reduce creasing which means less ironing.

Bizarre Britain

In Hinton St George, Somerset, children carry a hollowed-out Mangold Wurzel with a lit candle inside called a Punkie. Led around the village in procession by the Punkie King and Queen, it's thought the tradition comes from ancient times when village wives would take lanterns to search for their drunk husbands lost on the way home from Chiselborough Fair.

Portrait of a star

JANE FONDA

BORN: **December 21, 1937**
KNOWN FOR: **Barbarella, On Golden Pond, Barefoot In The Park, 9 to 5**
SHE SAID: **"When you can't remember why you're hurt, that's when you're healed."**

Recipe of the week

CHEDDAR AND POTATO SOUP

Serves: 4 Preparation time: 15 mins Cooking time: 1 hour

2 medium floury potatoes, scrubbed
¼ small onion, sliced
1 tsp oil
480ml (16floz) skimmed milk
40g (1½oz) cheddar cheese, grated
½ tsp dried dill
½ tsp dried rosemary
½ tsp salt
55g (2oz) bacon, chopped into small pieces
Few sprigs fresh dill

1 Preheat the oven to 180°C/350°F/Gas Mark 4. Bake the potatoes for 1 hour until soft inside, wrap in foil and turn oven off.

2 Fry onion in the oil until soft, but not brown. Roughly chop one of the potatoes and place in a food processor with the milk, cheese, onion, dill, rosemary and salt; blend until smooth.

3 Pour the soup into a pan, cook on a medium heat for 5 mins, season with pepper. Meanwhile, fry the bacon pieces until crispy.

4 Roughly chop the remaining baked potato. Serve topped with potato, bacon and sprigs of dill.
Lakeland

28 SUNDAY

29 MONDAY

30 TUESDAY

31 WEDNESDAY

1 THURSDAY

2 FRIDAY

3 SATURDAY

Blast from the past

The office party

Fifty years ago, the best office job in Southampton was with the Southern Gas Board. There were hundreds of us girls, mostly in our teens and twenties. When we joined we had to open a bank account to have our money paid in. A friend and I would often pop into our local branch around the 19th of the month to see if our money was in. The bank clerk would call out: "It isn't in yet!" - much to our dismay when we wanted to hit the shops at the weekend.

We would pay our keep to our mums and have a bit to spend, then a couple of lean weeks would follow. I got a part-time job in a pub for a few nights a week to save for driving lessons.

We had great office parties at Christmas. At first, drink was supplied but that stopped after a while as some people got too much in the festive spirit! We used to have a variety show featuring anyone on the staff who had a bit of talent. I particularly remember one year when the School of Navigation at Warsash sent a coach for us girls to go to their Christmas party - and it didn't cost us a penny!

Christine Young, Southampton

No 1 this week

1976 ABBA: Dancing Queen
The most commercially successful pop group of the Seventies, ABBA shot to fame after winning the Eurovision Song Contest in 1974. Although Waterloo, the song that won them the title, was a hit in the UK, the band initially struggled to shake off the stigma of Eurovision. In 1975 Mama Mia stormed the charts and was followed by a remarkable run of 18 consecutive top ten UK singles, including eight No.1s. Dancing Queen perfectly captured the disco period and remains a popular song today. In 2008 Meryl Streep released a version from the Mama Mia film soundtrack.

What a good idea

Love beans but not so fond of their after-effects? Try this clever tip of adding just a pinch of bicarbonate of soda to your pan of baked beans while they cook. A pinch won't be enough for you to taste it, but the bicarbonate of soda will reduce their wind-producing properties!

Bizarre Britain

Winter officially arrives in the Pennine hamlet of Langsett, with the Langsett Night of the Hunter's Moon. Always held on the Saturday night nearest the full moon before November 5, called the Hunter's Moon, this is when Mr Fox and his dancing entourage of mysterious cloaked figures, carrying flaming torches, take to the streets for a night of pagan revelry.

Portrait of a star

JUDY GARLAND

BORN: **June 10, 1922**
DIED: **June 22, 1969**
KNOWN FOR: **The Wizard Of Oz, A Star Is Born, Meet Me In St Louis, Easter Parade**
SHE SAID: **"Always be a first-rate version of yourself, instead of a second-rate version of somebody else."**

Recipe of the week

PUMPKIN PIE

Serves: 6-8 Preparation: 30 mins Cooking time: 40 mins

320g (11oz) ready-to-roll short crust pastry
425g (14oz) canned pumpkin
140g (5oz) caster sugar
½ tsp ground nutmeg
½ tsp ground cinnamon
2 eggs, beaten
25g (1oz) butter, melted
100g (4oz) Greek style yogurt
A sprinkle of ground cinnamon

1. Preheat the oven to 180°C/350°F/Gas Mark 4. Roll out the pastry on to a floured surface, and line a 22cm (9in) fluted, loose-bottom tart tin with the pastry. Place in the fridge for 10 mins.
2. Remove the pastry case from the fridge and line with a sheet of parchment paper and baking beans. Bake the pastry for 15-20 mins, then remove the paper and beans and cook for a further 5 mins. Remove from the oven and leave to cool.
3. In a bowl combine the pumpkin purée, caster sugar and spices, then beat in the eggs, melted butter and yogurt.
4. Pour the mixture into the tart and cook for 35-40 mins until the filling has just set.
5. Leave to cool, then remove the pie from the tin.

Rachel's Organic Yogurt

4 SUNDAY

5 MONDAY

6 TUESDAY

7 WEDNESDAY

8 THURSDAY

9 FRIDAY

10 SATURDAY

Blast from the past

Our bubble car

When I met my husband, Brian, in 1962 he had a Triumph motorbike – which was great as long as the weather was dry! Later, he sold it and bought a red Trojan bubble car which you could drive with a motorbike licence. It had a front opening door, folding sunshine roof and no reverse gear.

In his new car, off we went for a Sunday drive around the country lanes even though it was snowing hard. Suddenly the car spun round and blocked the lane. We couldn't open the door as it was stuck in the hedge. The only way out was through the roof. I couldn't manage to get out because I was wearing stiletto heels and a mini skirt so Brian climbed out and went to find a farm.

The farmer kindly came and helped him to lift the car and turn it round. By then there were quite a few cars waiting to come past. Luckily, no damage was done and we continued on our way.

We had the bubble car for two years before Brian took his driving test and was licensed to drive a four-wheeled vehicle.
Jeanette Young, Bromsgrove

No 1 this week

1960 Elvis Presley: It's Now or Never
Based on the Italian ballad, O Sole Mio which was popularised by Enrico Caruso, It's Now or Never was actually inspired by There's No Tomorrow, Tony Martin's interpretation of the same song. Presley was serving in the US Army in Germany when he first heard the track and, when he was discharged, returned to record it. The Jordanaires, Presley's long-time collaborators, provide the harmonies, accompanied by some very Italian-sounding instrumentation. In 2005, 28 years after Elvis' death, the song was re-released and reached the No.1 spot again.

What a good idea

If you've reached the last few drops of your favourite perfume, pour the remainder into an old unscented moisturiser or shower cream and mix or shake together. This way, you get to enjoy your lovely perfume for longer and you get a new, free, beautifully scented beauty product out of it.

Bizarre Britain

While most places remember Guy Fawkes on November 5, the villagers of Shebbear in Devon prepare to turn the Devil's Stone. No one quite knows where the strange six foot, tonne-heavy stone came from but labouring to turn it around is said to keep Shebbear safe from harm for the coming year.

Portrait of a star

TIPPI HEDREN

BORN: **January 19, 1930**
KNOWN FOR: **The Birds, Marnie, Roar, I Heart Huckabees**
SHE SAID: **"To be the object of somebody's obsession is a really awful feeling when you can't return it."**

Recipe of the week

SWEET CHILLI WELSH LAMB

Serves: 2 Preparation time: 5 mins Cooking time: 10 mins

5ml (1 tsp) sesame oil
15ml (1 tbsp) olive oil
450g (1lb) Welsh lamb steaks, cut into thin strips
1 clove garlic, crushed
3 tbsp sweet chilli sauce
1 lime, juice and rind
100g (4oz) sugar snap peas or mangetout, sliced
225g (8oz) pre-cooked noodles
4 spring onions, thinly sliced
30g (2 tbsp) fresh coriander, chopped

1 Heat the oils in a large non-stick frying pan or wok, add the lamb strips and garlic.
2 Cook for 4-5 mins until meat is browned on all sides and cooked through.
3 Add the sweet chilli sauce and cook for 1-2 mins.
4 Add the lime juice and rind, sugar snap peas or mangetout and stir through.
5 Add the noodles and spring onions, toss together and serve scattered with coriander.
www.eatwelshlambandbeef.com

11 SUNDAY

12 MONDAY

13 TUESDAY

14 WEDNESDAY

15 THURSDAY

16 FRIDAY

17 SATURDAY

Blast from the past

Party fun and games

This photo must have been taken around 1956 when I was nine years old and my dad was stationed at RAF Laarbruch in Germany. The boys sitting on the sledge were our next-door neighbours, David, Michael and Peter Skelton. Every week we swapped our comics over the garden fence, but we couldn't exchange my Girl and School Friend for their Eagle and Beano until our fathers had read them first!

While older children went away to boarding school, we attended the primary school on the camp. David and I were in the same class and had a marvellous teacher called Miss Peacock. She loved being with children and happily joined in the fun when my mother invited her to my birthday party. In those simpler times, the fun consisted of games such as pinning the tail on the donkey (you had to wear a blindfold and not cheat by peeping) as well as that perennial favourite, pass the parcel. Another game was seeing who could remember the most objects on a tray after it had been covered over.

The highlight for me was blowing out the candles on the cake in one go so that I could make a special birthday wish.
Marion Reeve, Norfolk

No 1 this week

1983 Billy Joel: **Uptown Girl**
When interviewed Billy Joel said the song, which he had originally titled Uptown Girls, was written on an occasion when he was surrounded by beautiful models including his then-girlfriend Elle Macpherson. The video featured Joel as a motor mechanic, sighing over his pin-up, who then turns up in a vintage Rolls-Royce. Supermodel Christie Brinkley stars in the video and many people assumed the song was about her - especially as the pair later married. Uptown Girl was Billy Joel's only No.1 in the UK.

What a good idea

If you'd like to lose a few pounds or just get a little fitter, don't wait for the New Year to make a resolution. Gym memberships are usually at their cheapest just after the post-summer slump and before the January rush to get fit begins, so it's best to sign up now.

Bizarre Britain

Stand well back on the streets of Hatherleigh, Devon as the yearly carnival parade of blazing tar barrels - a custom dating back to ancient times - comes through the market town at 5am. Interestingly the carnival's other main attraction is a procession of crêpe paper tableaux - let's just hope they don't end up anywhere near the blazing tar barrels!

Portrait of a star

DORIS DAY

BORN: **April 3, 1924**
KNOWN FOR: **Pillow Talk, Calamity Jane, The Man Who Knew Too Much, Send Me No Flowers**
SHE SAID: **"The really frightening thing about middle age is the knowledge that you'll grow out of it."**

Recipe of the week

MALTED MILK CHOCOLATE TRAYBAKE

Serves: 16 Preparation time: 30 mins Cooking time: 30 mins

75g (3oz) walnuts
175g (6oz) plain flour
¼ tsp baking powder
¼ tsp bicarbonate of soda
2 tbsp malted milk powder
Pinch of salt
175g (6oz) butter
225g (8oz) light muscovado sugar
3 lightly beaten eggs
2 tsp vanilla extract
75g (3oz) halved Maltesers
175ml (6floz) double cream
1 tbsp maple syrup
125g (4½oz) 54-68 per cent dark chocolate
125g (4½oz) milk chocolate
125g (4½oz) butter

1 Preheat oven 170°C/325°F/Gas Mark 3. Lightly toast the walnuts for 5 mins. Roughly chop, leave to cool.

2 Sift together the flour, baking powder, bicarbonate of soda, malted milk powder and salt.

3 In a separate bowl, cream the butter and sugar until pale and light. Gradually add the eggs and vanilla extract.

4 Fold in dry ingredients until well mixed, add the Maltesers and walnuts.

5 Bake in a 23cm (9in) square tray, greased and lined, on the middle shelf for 20-25 mins. Leave to cool.

6 Heat the double cream and maple syrup until just boiling. Pour over the dark chocolate and milk chocolate. Add the butter, leave to melt. Stir until smooth. Remove from pan and spread chocolate on top. Decorate.

From Brownies, Blondies & Other Traybakes by Ryland Peters & Small, £14.99

18 SUNDAY

19 MONDAY

20 TUESDAY

21 WEDNESDAY

22 THURSDAY

23 FRIDAY

24 SATURDAY

Blast from the past

Sweet shop memories

My mum, Vera Fern, wrote her memories to pass on to her children and grandchildren. Here's an extract of her recollections of shopping:

'Before supermarkets shopkeepers took such a pride in their shops. Sometimes it took them all day to dress their windows. Grocers had their goods delivered in bulk. A side of bacon which had to be boned and then put on a machine to be sliced. Lard and cheese came in big blocks which had to be cut into small portions and wrapped. Sugar and dried fruit had to be weighed into pounds and bagged up.

'There was a sweet shop in our High Street which made its own sweets. There was a huge steel table in the middle of the shop where you could watch the owner making them, rolling out this mixture and then cutting it up to put in these jars all around the shop. The children were in awe watching him, mouths watering.

'I left school when I was 14 and went to work in a department store. I had an interview and was given a test to see if you could add up. The tills did not add up in those days, you had to do it all in your head. We had to be on the shop floor by 8.50am and the manager had us all line up for inspection - looking smart with clean nails and not too much jewellery'.
Linda Mundy, by email

No 1 this week

1979 Dr Hook: When You're in Love with A Beautiful Woman
Dr Hook had an eclectic catalogue of success with chart hits covering everything from disco, soft-rock, acoustic ballads and novelty songs. Originally called Dr Hook & The Medicine Show, the Hook name was inspired by the Peter Pan pirate because of singer Ray Sawyer's eye patch (he lost his eye in a car accident in 1967). When You're in Love with A Beautiful Woman was written by Even Stevens and first appeared on the 1978 album Pleasure and Pain.

What a good idea

Fed up of seeing dust gather quickly around your house? Douse and wring out a soft cloth or a duster in a little white vinegar and then wipe all the hard surfaces around your house with this. The white vinegar is great at stopping dust settling, meaning you won't have to go around dusting quite so often.

Bizarre Britain

Pinocchio would have a field day in Santon Bridge, Cumbria, which hosts the World's Biggest Liar Competition. Held in memory of Will Ritson, a famous Cumbrian known for his tall tales – he told people the turnips in nearby Wasdale were so big they had be quarried – competitors get five minutes to tell the most convincing lie they can.

Portrait of a star

GARY COOPER

BORN: **May 7, 1901**
DIED: **May 13, 1961**
KNOWN FOR: **High Noon, Sergeant York, Mr Deeds Goes To Town**
HE SAID: **"Until I came along all the leading men were handsome, but luckily they wrote a lot of stories about the fellow next door."**

Recipe of the week

CHICKEN AND CHICKPEA TAGINE

Serves: 2 Preparation time: 10 mins Cooking time: 14 mins

1 tbsp olive oil
150g (5oz) chicken breast, diced
1 onion, chopped
2 tsp harissa paste
75g (3oz) dried apricots, roughly chopped
400g (14oz) can chickpeas, drained and rinsed
400g (14oz) can chopped tomatoes
1 tbsp chopped parsley or coriander
100g (3½oz) wholewheat couscous

1 Heat the oil in a saucepan and fry the chicken and onion for 3 mins to brown. Add the harissa paste and cook for 1 min.

2 Stir in the apricots, chickpeas and tomatoes. Fill the tomato can to half way with water and add to the pan. Simmer for 10 mins until the chicken is cooked through with no pink meat. Season and stir in the herbs.

3 Meanwhile, place the couscous in a small bowl and pour over enough boiling water to just cover. Cover the bowl with cling film and leave for 5 mins before fluffing up with a fork. Serve with the tagine.

www.waitrose.com/recipes

25 SUNDAY

26 MONDAY

27 TUESDAY

28 WEDNESDAY

29 THURSDAY

30 FRIDAY

1 SATURDAY

Blast from the past
The greatest grotto

This is me, aged around five years old, after visiting Lewis' department store in Leicester. It would have been in the early Sixties and around that time all my school friends wanted to visit Santa at Lewis' because they had the best grotto in town.

This year was particularly special because my dad took me. On the way to see Santa we stopped to look in the department store window. Lewis' always put on a good show but this year they'd surpassed themselves – with the most incredible wonderland of festive scenes with moving figures – to a five year old it appeared magical.

Every child in the city seemed to be there with their noses pressed against the window, dreaming about which one of the gifts on display might find its way into their stocking.

The queue to see Santa was always massive but the chatter and excitement all added to the anticipation. At the end of the grotto there was always a photo opportunity with Muffin the Mule – there was a different themed backdrop each year but I think virtually everyone who grew up in Leicester in the Sixties will have a photograph very like this one. Sadly, despite local public protest, the Lewis' store was demolished in 1994 – but the memories remain.
Judith Allen, Leicester

No 1 this week

1975 Queen: Bohemian Rhapsody
The UK's third biggest-selling single of all time, Bohemian Rhapsody has actually topped the UK charts twice, first for nine weeks in 1975/6 and then again for five weeks in 1991 following Freddie Mercury's death. Queen are also the only band to achieve the Christmas No.1 slot twice with the same song. In 2004, the song was inducted into the Grammy Hall of Fame and in 2012, it topped a nationwide poll to find the UK's favourite No.1.

What a good idea

As you're wrapping up the Christmas presents, stop wrapping paper unhelpfully unrolling by cutting a toilet roll lengthwise and wrapping it around the roll to keep it in place. To stop you getting backache as you reach down and wrap on the floor, you may also find wrapping on an ironing board, adjusted to your height, is much better.

Bizarre Britain

Legend has it that in the 19th Century, the baby heir to Culverthorpe Hall, Lincolnshire was tossed from a window by the family's pet ape. Years later, locals remember the story with the Oasby Baboon Tossing Night where a man in a monkey costume is pursued by torchlight and a toy monkey tossed over the roof of the local pub.

Portrait of a star

VIVIEN LEIGH

BORN: **November 5, 1913**
DIED: **July 8, 1967**
KNOWN FOR: **Gone With The Wind, A Streetcar Named Desire, Waterloo Bridge**
SHE SAID: **"Most of us have compromised with life. Those who fight for what they want will always thrill us."**

Recipe of the week

SAUSAGE AND RATATOUILLE CASSEROLE

Serves: 4 Preparation time: 10 mins Cooking time: 25 mins

454g (16oz) 8-pack British pork sausages
400g (14oz) new potatoes, diced
400g (14oz) chopped tomatoes
390g (14oz) can Waitrose Ratatouille Provençale
25g (1oz) fresh flat-leaf parsley, chopped

1 Place the sausages under a preheated grill for 15 mins, turning occasionally. Cut into thick slices once cooked.

2 Meanwhile, cook the potatoes in boiling water for 10 mins until tender, drain and return to the pan. Add the tomatoes and ratatouille and simmer for 5 mins.

3 Stir in the sausages and cook for 2-3 mins. Sprinkle over the parsley and serve.

www.waitrose.com/recipes

2 SUNDAY

3 MONDAY

4 TUESDAY

5 WEDNESDAY

6 THURSDAY

7 FRIDAY

8 SATURDAY

Blast from the past
Home for Christmas

When I was 11 years old I had to go into the Elizabeth Garrett Anderson hospital in Bloomsbury to have my tonsils and adenoids removed. I missed my family, hated the food and hated the injections I had to have every day. Whenever my dad came to visit me, I'd cry and ask him to take me home.

Then one morning some people arrived and started decorating the ward for Christmas. Mrs Dale from the radio show, Mrs Dale's Diary, arrived with an enormous box of chocolates which we were told we could open on Christmas Eve. There was talk of Father Christmas coming and a pantomime to be performed by the nurses and doctors. I began to think I might enjoy Christmas in hospital after all.

That evening Dad arrived with a big smile and said he had convinced the doctors to let me come home. We travelled by public transport in a thick, pea-souper fog. The next day Dad came down with an awful attack of bronchitis. We spent the holiday very quietly, trying not to disturb him. I was so sad to miss out on Father Christmas, the pantomime and especially Mrs Dale's chocolates!
Ann Rowe, London

No 1 this week

1961 Frankie Vaughan: Tower of Strength
Written by Burt Bacharach and Bob Hilliard Tower of Strength was originally performed by Gene McDaniels in 1961. Frankie Vaughan released his version of the song later in the same year and took it to No.1. The B-side was a cover of Al Martino's Rachel. The Liverpudlian singer recorded more than 80 singles in his lifetime and was often known as Mr Moonlight, after one of his early hits. In 1994, he was one of a few to be honoured by a second appearance on This Is Your Life, when he was surprised by Michael Aspel.

What a good idea

Deck the halls with homemade baubles! If you're keen to jazz up the Christmas tree this year try making your own decorations. Styrofoam balls, covered with sequins, stuck in with straight pins and a blob of glue on the underneath are simple to make. Old light bulbs, painted and accessorised look lovely, too, as do pinecones dusted in glitter.

Bizarre Britain

Each December, specially minted coins are distributed in the Town Hall of Richmond, Yorkshire, in a custom dating back to the 16th Century, when donations of a shilling were given to the needy in the run-up to Christmas. Knowing that a shilling doesn't buy you much today, recipients now receive a special coin marked with an image of Richmond Castle.

Portrait of a star

PAUL NEWMAN

BORN: **January 26, 1925**
DIED: **September 26, 2008**
KNOWN FOR: **Cool Hand Luke, Butch Cassidy and The Sundance Kid, The Sting**
HE SAID: **"People stay married because they want to, not because the doors are locked."**

Recipe of the week

CRANBERRY MERINGUES

Serves: 6 Preparation time: 10 mins Cooking time: None

75g (3oz) cranberries
4 tbsp maple syrup
6 ready-made meringue nests
200ml ($^1/_3$pt) double or whipping cream
Zest and juice of 1 lime

1 Place the cranberries and maple syrup in a pan. Heat gently until the syrup begins to bubble but don't let the cranberries pop. Once the cranberries are softened, place them in a bowl and set aside until cold, stirring to keep them evenly coated in syrup.

2 To serve, place the meringue nests on individual serving plates. Whip the cream to soft peaks and stir in the lime juice and zest. Place a few of the prepared and chilled cranberries in the base of each meringue, then spoon on a little cream and top with more of the cranberries. Serve immediately.

www.berryworld.com

9 SUNDAY

10 MONDAY

11 TUESDAY

12 WEDNESDAY

13 THURSDAY

14 FRIDAY

15 SATURDAY

Blast from the past

A snowy surprise

When I was aged nine, I was very disappointed when it didn't snow on the morning of Christmas Day. We spent Christmas at my grandfather's house in Surrey. He was a widower so his housekeeper, Nell, cooked the dinner.

As the crackers were supposed to contain some indoor fireworks, we pulled a few of them as soon as we sat down at the table. Talk about a damp squib! They were very disappointing and the adults all grumbled about what a waste of money they had been.

If only we had looked upwards, we would have seen a cloud of artificial snow produced by the fireworks settled across the ceiling. As Dad carved the turkey, hundreds of 'snowflakes' began to fall, settling on our food. Nell and Mum shrieked and grabbed the napkins to cover our plates while Grandpa uttered some more colourful comments! We managed to rescue the meal and enjoyed our festive fare despite the unexpected white Christmas that we hadn't been dreaming of!

The photo is of me with Father Christmas at a department store in Reading. I was an avid reader and thrilled that my presents included the Observer Book of Birds which I still have today.
Pat Gannon-Leary, Gateshead

No 1 this week

1963 The Beatles: I Want to Hold Your Hand
With advance orders exceeding one million copies, The Beatles' I Want to Hold Your Hand would have gone straight to the top of the UK record charts on its day of release (November 29, 1963) had it not been blocked by the group's one million-seller She Loves You, their previous UK single, which was having a resurgence of popularity following intense media coverage of the group. It took I Want to Hold Your Hand two weeks to dislodge its predecessor, but it stayed at No.1 for five weeks and remained in the UK top 50 for 21 weeks in total.

What a good idea

The Christmas party season may lead to a few late nights in a row. To reduce puffiness and redness around your eyes, don't opt for an expensive cream but instead use cooled, used green tea bags left on your eyes for 15 minutes. You'll soon look fresh-faced and ready for the next round of festivities.

Bizarre Britain

Saturnalia was a popular Roman midwinter festival lasting seven days, celebrating the god of agriculture, Saturn, in hopes of prosperity to come. It was a time to eat, drink and be merry, and in Chester locals still practise this ancient festival with a torch-lit parade of Roman centurions with dancers and entertainers as well as rites to Saturn himself.

Portrait of a star

STEVE MCQUEEN

BORN: **March 24, 1930**
DIED: **November 7, 1980**
KNOWN FOR: **Bullitt, The Great Escape, The Magnificent Seven, The Getaway**
HE SAID: **"You only go around once in life and I'm going to grab a handful of it."**

Recipe of the week

SCOTCH EGG PIE

Serves: 6 Preparation time: 15 mins Cooking time: 45 mins

7 free range eggs
450g (1lb) pork sausagemeat
6 sundried tomatoes, finely chopped
6 salad onions, thinly sliced
2 tbsp grated Parmigiano Reggiano
25g (1oz) flat-leaf parsley, finely chopped
2 x 215g (7oz) all-butter puff pastry sheets
1 tbsp Dijon mustard
Plain flour, for dusting

1 Preheat the oven to 200°C/400°F/Gas Mark 6. Cook 6 of the eggs in a pan of boiling water for 6-8 mins. Cool and remove the shells.

2 Mix together the sausagemeat, sundried tomatoes, salad onions, Parmigiano Reggiano and parsley until well blended.

3 Open out one sheet of the pastry and place on a baking sheet. Spread with Dijon mustard then smooth a third of the sausage mixture over the pastry, leaving a 1cm (½in) border around the edges. Place the peeled eggs, evenly spaced, on the sausagemeat then cover with the remaining mixture to enclose them.

4 Roll out the second sheet of pastry on a floured surface to make it a little larger. Beat the remaining egg and brush along the borders of the pastry, then lay the second sheet of pastry over the filling. Use a fork to press the borders together firmly to seal into a neat rectangular pie, trimming the edges if necessary.

5 Brush the pie with beaten egg and bake for 40 mins until golden and cooked through. Leave to cool for a few minutes before slicing.

www.waitrose.com

16 SUNDAY

17 MONDAY

18 TUESDAY

19 WEDNESDAY

20 THURSDAY

21 FRIDAY

22 SATURDAY

Blast from the past

Ghost of Christmas past

I am now 93 years old and remember Christmases being great fun when I was a child. Our family (my parents and my two sisters) stayed at my grandparents' house. Four of my grandmother's seven children were married and two of our cousins lived next door so there were about twenty of us altogether.

We often slept five in a bed, lying sideways so there was more room. In the morning we all had a stocking containing small gifts. After breakfast Santa Claus came with a sack of gifts. The children sat at a small table for dinner while aunts, uncles and grandparents sat at a big table. Granddad would carve the huge turkey and joint of beef and there were silver gifts to be found in the pudding.

After lunch we would go to the best room where one of our aunties would play the piano and we all sang - and often fall asleep! We had sandwiches and cake for tea in front of the fire. Our uncles often used to play tricks on my grandparents. Our aunts used to take us out for walks. It was wonderful to be with my cousins. Christmas will never be like that again.
Marion Ward, Colchester

No 1 this week

1977 Wings: Mull of Kintyre
Paul McCartney wrote Mull of Kintyre with his Wings bandmate Denny Laine. The song is a tribute to the picturesque peninsula in Scotland where Paul and his wife, Linda, had a farm. The song was Wings' biggest hit in the UK, became the 1977 Christmas No.1 and stayed there for nine weeks. It also became the first UK single to sell more than two million copies. In 2014 Susan Boyle performed the song at the opening ceremony of the Commonwealth Games.

What a good idea

As turkey breasts cook faster than the rest of the bird, making the meat dry, avoid overcooking by placing a bag of ice cubes on to the breasts for half an hour before cooking. Then coat the whole bird with vegetable oil and cover with foil before roasting in the oven.

Bizarre Britain

Broughton, Northamptonshire is normally a haven of quiet. But come December all that changes when the raucous custom of the Tin Can Band disturbs the peace. Intended to drive away evil spirits, villagers make a racket with pans, kettles and whistles, beginning on the stroke of midnight and ending with a chorus of Auld Lang Syne at the church gates.

Portrait of a star

KIRK DOUGLAS

BORN: **December 9, 1916**
KNOWN FOR: **Spartacus, Paths of Glory, 20,000 Leagues Under the Sea**
HE SAID: **"In order to achieve anything you must be brave enough to fail."**

Recipe of the week

CLEMENTINE AND WALNUT MINCE PIE

Serves: 12 Preparation time: 20 mins
Cooking time: 15-20 mins

200g (7oz) plain flour, plus extra for dusting
100g (3½oz) cold butter, cubed
25g (1oz) ground almonds
50g (2oz) icing sugar
1 medium egg, beaten
75g (3oz) walnuts
1 Cox apple, peeled, cored and coarsely grated
200g (7oz) vegetarian mincemeat
1 clementine, peeled and diced
1-2 tbsp Grand Marnier liqueur
For the icing:
125g (4½oz) icing sugar, plus extra
Juice ½ clementine

1 Preheat the oven to 200°C/400°F/Gas Mark 6. Whizz the flour, butter, ground almonds, icing sugar and egg in a food processor until the pastry comes together. Wrap the pastry in clingfilm and chill for about 30 mins.

2 Toast the walnuts on a tray in the oven for 4-5 mins until golden. Allow to cool then roughly chop.

3 Mix three-quarters of the walnuts with the grated apple, mincemeat, clementine and Grand Marnier.

4 Roll out the pastry until 3mm thick. Using a 9cm (3½in) pastry cutter, stamp out 12 rounds and use to line a 12-hole muffin tin. Fill each case with mincemeat mix.

5 Bake the pies for 10-12 mins. Cool for 5 mins, then transfer to a wire rack to cool completely.

6 To make the icing, mix the icing sugar with enough clementine juice to make a smooth paste. Drizzle icing over each mince pie, sprinkle with the reserved walnuts.

www.waitrose.com

23 SUNDAY

24 MONDAY

25 TUESDAY

26 WEDNESDAY

27 THURSDAY

28 FRIDAY

29 SATURDAY

Blast from the past

Spirit of the Blitz

My first day at work was on Monday, December 30th, 1940 and, unknown to me, the night before London had suffered one of its worst air raids ever.

Aged 14, I was up early and dressed in my new coat and hat and first pair of stockings. Feeling nervous and excited, I caught the train from Dagenham with all the other workers, but we were told to alight at Bow Road. No one knew what was happening so I followed the crowd out of the station and got on to a lorry that went as far as Aldgate, where again we had to get off. A girl asked me where I was going and when I told her 'Liverpool Street', she said she knew where that was. When we came to her place of work it was nowhere near Liverpool Street so I retraced my steps and asked a policeman the way.

When I reported to the desk and apologised for being late, I was assured that I wasn't the only one that day. Then I was told to go upstairs and clean up which I thought was a bit cheeky until I looked in the mirror. To my horror, my hair was wet and straight, my face streaked black, and my new stockings laddered!

Audrey Ward, Suffolk

No 1 this week

1966 Tom Jones: Green, Green Grass of Home
Although originally a country song first recorded by Johnny Darrell, Tom Jones was inspired to record his own version after hearing a Jerry Lee Lewis cover. The Welsh singer had been staying in New York City because he was scheduled to appear on the Ed Sullivan Show and visited Colony Records, where he first heard the track. When released in the UK it took the 1966 Christmas No.1 slot and stayed there for a total of seven weeks.

What a good idea

If you've got a bottle of bubbly on the go for Christmas and New Year and want it to stay fresh for longer, try dropping a couple of raisins into the bottle. The sugar in the raisins helps reinvigorate the bubbles and works with all sparkling wines, Champagne and prosecco.

Bizarre Britain

Every Boxing Day, the Grenoside Sword Dancers of Sheffield, perform a unique sword dance while wearing clogs. The dance has been around for at least 150 years and the routine usually features a ritual 'beheading' of their captain near the beginning of the dance. They perform by carrying the swords between them in an unbroken chain.

Portrait of a star

JAYNE MANSFIELD

BORN: **April 19, 1933**
DIED: **June 29, 1967**
KNOWN FOR: **The Girl Can't Help It, Will Success Spoil Rock Hunter?, Too Hot To Handle**
SHE SAID: **"If you're going to do something wrong, do it big, because the punishment is the same either way."**

Recipe of the week

PLUM CHUTNEY

Serves 6: Preparation time: 15 mins Cooking time: 25 mins

250g (9oz) red plums
250g (9oz) yellow plums
100g (3½oz) shallots, finely chopped
2 tbsp vegetable oil
3 star anise
1 tsp cardamom pods, crushed
1 tsp coriander seeds
60g (2½oz) caster sugar
260ml (9floz) cider vinegar

1 Chop the plums into 8 pieces, discarding the stones. Place a pan over a medium heat and sweat the shallots with the oil and spices until soft and caramelised. Add the chopped plums, sugar and vinegar.

2 Cook on a low heat, stirring occasionally, until the plums are soft. Make sure not to caramelise them. Cook for approximately 25 mins.

3 Remove from the heat and allow to cool. This chutney will keep in the fridge for up to 3 days, or pour into sterilised jars for a longer shelf life.
www.waitrose.com

30 SUNDAY

31 MONDAY

1 TUESDAY

2 WEDNESDAY

3 THURSDAY

4 FRIDAY

5 SATURDAY

Blast from the past
Our precious firstborn

On December 11, 1964, our son Andrew was born six months premature, weighing just three pounds. He was put in an incubator and before my husband, Tom, and I could see him we had to put on caps, cotton gowns, plastic gloves and plastic covers on our shoes. Only then were we allowed into the room with big glass windows through which we could see our son.

I was allowed to go home on Christmas Eve. After dinner on Christmas Day, we went to see Andrew, but found that his incubator was empty! My heart sank to my boots and we looked at each other in alarm. A nurse said: "Don't look so worried, we have moved Andrew to another room."

She took us to the room where he was lying in a cot, breathing on his own! The nurse asked if I would like to hold him and she handed him to me. I had tears in my eyes and when I looked at Tom, his eyes were glistening, too. Holding my son was the best Christmas present I ever had.

On January 21, 1965, in the snow, we took Andrew home. This photo was taken when he was twelve weeks old.
Yvonne Parsons, Exmouth

No 1 this week

1952 Al Martino: Here in My Heart
Al Martino's recording of Here in My Heart made history as the first ever No.1 in the UK singles chart. It remained at the top spot for nine weeks, setting a record for the longest consecutive run at No.1, a record which, over the following 50 years, has only been beaten by six other tracks. Al had six further UK chart hits and headlined at the London Palladium. Al Martino is also remembered for his role of Johnny Fontane in The Godfather film trilogy.

What a good idea

As you pack away your Christmas decs for another year, think about storing them differently to save you opening up the box to tangles and breakages next time. Use plastic cups to neatly store the bigger ornaments and egg cartons for the smaller, more-fiddly items. Wrap your Christmas lights around a clothes hanger.

Bizarre Britain

Stonehaven, Aberdeenshire welcomes in the New Year with a procession of 45 brave folk who whirl blazing fireballs around their heads on long wires. Carried down the streets from midnight, these fireballs are then thrown into the sea. The tradition may come from the ancient belief fire purifies the streets, encouraging the sun to return after midwinter.

Portrait of a star

MAUREEN O'HARA

BORN: **August 17, 1920**
DIED: **October 24, 2015**
KNOWN FOR: **The Quiet Man, How Green Was My Valley, Miracle On 34th Street**
SHE SAID: **"I have never lost my faith in God. God has a most wicked sense of humour."**

Recipe of the week

TURKEY MEATBALLS IN TOMATO SAUCE

Serves: 4 Preparation time: 20 mins Cooking time: 20 mins

For the meatballs:
1 tbsp of melted coconut oil
800g (1lb 7oz) British turkey breast mince
1 onion, finely diced
1 small red pepper, finely diced
1 clove garlic, minced
2 tbsp chopped fresh organic parsley
Pinch of sea salt and fresh pepper
2 free-range eggs
For the sauce:
1 onion, finely chopped
2 tbsp coconut oil
1 tsp sea salt
1 crushed garlic clove
1 tsp dried thyme
1 tsp of oregano
2 cans chopped tomatoes

1 Preheat oven to 180°C/350°F/Gas Mark 4. Place all the meatball ingredients in a medium bowl and mix everything together. Roll into 1½in balls.

2 For the sauce fry the onion in a little coconut oil and salt. After 5 mins add the rest of the ingredients. Cook for 10 mins.

3 Place the meatballs on a roasting tray, evenly spaced and pour over the sauce. Bake for 20 mins. Serve with pasta.
www.britishturkey.co.uk

2018 year-to-view calender

JANUARY

M	1	8	15	22	29	
Tu	2	9	16	23	30	
W	3	10	17	24	31	
Th	4	11	18	25		
F	5	12	19	26		
Sa	6	13	20	27		
Su	7	14	21	28		

FEBRUARY

M		5	12	19	26	
Tu		6	13	20	27	
W		7	14	21	28	
Th	1	8	15	22		
F	2	9	16	23		
Sa	3	10	17	24		
Su	4	11	18	25		

MARCH

M		5	12	19	26	
Tu		6	13	20	27	
W		7	14	21	28	
Th	1	8	15	22	29	
F	2	9	16	23	30	
Sa	3	10	17	24	31	
Su	4	11	18	25		

APRIL

M		2	9	16	23	30
Tu		3	10	17	24	
W		4	11	18	25	
Th		5	12	19	26	
F		6	13	20	27	
Sa		7	14	21	28	
Su	1	8	15	22	29	

MAY

M		7	14	21	28	
Tu	1	8	15	22	29	
W	2	9	16	23	30	
Th	3	10	17	24	31	
F	4	11	18	25		
Sa	5	12	19	26		
Su	6	13	20	27		

JUNE

M		4	11	18	25	
Tu		5	12	19	26	
W		6	13	20	27	
Th		7	14	21	28	
F	1	8	15	22	29	
Sa	2	9	16	23	30	
Su	3	10	17	24		

JULY

M		2	9	16	23	30
Tu		3	10	17	24	31
W		4	11	18	25	
Th		5	12	19	26	
F		6	13	20	27	
Sa		7	14	21	28	
Su	1	8	15	22	29	

AUGUST

M		6	13	20	27	
Tu		7	14	21	28	
W	1	8	15	22	29	
Th	2	9	16	23	30	
F	3	10	17	24	31	
Sa	4	11	18	25		
Su	5	12	19	26		

SEPTEMBER

M		3	10	17	24	
Tu		4	11	18	25	
W		5	12	19	26	
Th		6	13	20	27	
F		7	14	21	28	
Sa	1	8	15	22	29	
Su	2	9	16	23	30	

OCTOBER

M	1	8	15	22	29	
Tu	2	9	16	23	30	
W	3	10	17	24	31	
Th	4	11	18	25		
F	5	12	19	26		
Sa	6	13	20	27		
Su	7	14	21	28		

NOVEMBER

M		5	12	19	26	
Tu		6	13	20	27	
W		7	14	21	28	
Th	1	8	15	22	29	
F	2	9	16	23	30	
Sa	3	10	17	24		
Su	4	11	18	25		

DECEMBER

M		3	10	17	24	31
Tu		4	11	18	25	
W		5	12	19	26	
Th		6	13	20	27	
F		7	14	21	28	
Sa	1	8	15	22	29	
Su	2	9	16	23	30	

RELAX & UNWIND

Size doesn't

When Malcolm sets out to rekindle romance, his big gesture

Malcolm and Deirdre had been married for 40 years and, to all appearances, theirs was a successful marriage. They had raised four children, three of whom were now happily married themselves, and they had nine adorable grandchildren.

But appearances can be deceptive and an unseen tension lurked beneath their apparent ease as they sat reading in their living room. The grandfather clock struck ten and Malcolm sighed contentedly as he put down his book, A History of Modern Britain by Andrew Marr. He glanced across the room to where Deirdre was engrossed in her latest Mills and Boon romance. He thought to himself it was a pity he could not interest her in some more worthwhile reading matter.

"I think it's time for our cocoa and digestive biscuits," he said.

Deirdre sighed as she set her book aside and looked at Malcolm. How had they become so set in their ways? Where had all the excitement of their youth gone?

"That was a melancholy sigh," Malcolm said. "Is anything wrong? Would you rather have that last slice of Battenburg instead of a biscuit?"

"I really don't care what we have with our cocoa," Deirdre responded. "It's just - oh, I don't know, Malcolm. This book I'm reading...Well, what I mean is, when was the last time either of us did anything romantic?"

Malcolm was thoughtful while he made the cocoa. He supposed Deirdre was right. He was an overweight, balding headmaster - nothing like the handsome young fellows she liked to read about. In truth, he was rather a practical man who didn't like to waste money on unnecessary luxuries. His last gift to her had been a food processor. Perhaps, on reflection, that had been a mistake.

And now he thought about it, Deirdre had seemed down in the dumps since their youngest had left home to live in London. He decided that this year he would buy her something really personal and romantic for her birthday, which was coming up soon.

And so it was that the

He decided that this year he would buy her something really personal and romantic for her birthday, which was coming up soon

---

following week he found himself, much to his embarrassment, in the lingerie section of their nearest department store.

The attractive young assistant asked: "Can I help you?"

"Thank you. I'd like to see the prettiest nightdresses you have, please - and price is not an issue," he added hastily.

The assistant took him over to a display of dreamy, luxurious nightdresses. "These are all pure silk, sir. I can assure you that the fabric feels absolutely divine against the skin," she gushed.

Malcolm gazed in wonder at the beautiful garments, then gulped nervously when he read the attached price tags. His tremulous hand reached out towards a gorgeous black and red creation that was certainly very different from Deirdre's usual choice of nightwear.

"Is this a gift for a more mature lady?" the assistant enquired tactfully, adding: "Most people find that cream is a more flattering colour for women of a certain age."

"Oh, um, yes," stammered Malcolm. "Er - I'm sure you're right."

After some deliberation, he finally decided on a full-length cream silk nightdress trimmed with lace the colour of milky coffee. He felt sure this colour combination would please Deirdre as she had recently bought a camel coat of similar hue.

"An exquisite choice," enthused the assistant. "And do you know the lucky lady's dress size?"

"Certainly!" Malcolm replied confidently, now on more sure ground. "I'd like a size 12, please. And would you be so kind as to gift wrap it for me."

As he left the store carrying a bag containing a silver box adorned with a gold rosette

Words Heather Morris / Illustration Claire Fletcher

matter

has one small flaw...

box to hold it up against her, but as she did so the smile faded slowly away.

Malcolm was truly puzzled. "Don't you like it, dear?"

"It is lovely, dear, but I'm afraid it's the wrong size," she explained dejectedly.

"But it can't be," Malcolm remonstrated. "I distinctly remember on our honeymoon weekend in London you fell in love with that lacy nightie in Dickins and Jones and I bought it for you. It was definitely a size 12. I remember it well."

"Oh, Malcolm, dearest!" Deirdre replied. "That was many years ago - before I'd given birth to four children. I'm sorry, but these days I'm a size 18."

Malcolm was devastated to find that his romantic gesture had failed so miserably. He said: "But you are still that lovely young girl I married. You don't look any different to me and I love you even more now than I did then. I am so sorry, dear. What can I do to make amends?"

Deirdre said gently: "That is the most romantic thing you have ever said to me, Malcolm. Now, don't you worry, dear. We can have a lovely trip into town together tomorrow and I'm sure the shop won't mind changing it for one the right size."

"And afterwards we will go and have lunch at that nice Italian restaurant overlooking the river," he said.

That night, as they cuddled up close together, Malcolm in his striped pyjamas and Deirdre in her usual cotton nightie, they were indeed as romantic as they had been on their wedding night all those years ago - just as Malcolm had hoped.

within which the nightdress nestled in layers of tissue paper, there was an unaccustomed spring in Malcolm's step.

He hummed happily to himself as he waited for the bus home. This birthday gift was just the thing to cheer Deirdre up. What could be more romantic? He began to look forward to bedtime on his wife's birthday almost as much as he had anticipated their wedding night.

At last the day dawned and eagerly Malcolm presented Deirdre with the silver gift box. She gasped with surprise.

'It's obviously not going to be something for the house this time', she thought excitedly to herself. As she peeled back the layers of tissue to reveal the soft, silky garment, she was overcome with emotion.

Smiling with delight, she exclaimed: "Oh, Malcolm. This is just beautiful!" Tenderly, she drew the nightdress from the

Two-speed crossword

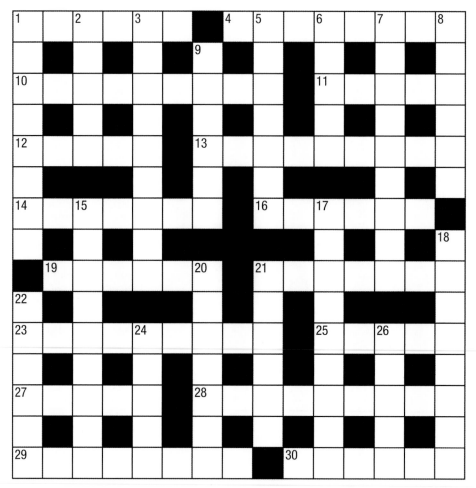

For this puzzle we've provided two sets of clues, each giving the same answers. Quick clues are below and Cryptic to the right. It's a good way to hone your skills, because it gives you two ways to crack the crossword!

ACROSS
1   Metamorphose (6)
4   Gigantic (8)
10 Cleaning product (9)
11 Pre-Euro coin (5)
12 Reigned (5)
13 Focus of attention (9)
14 Bee Gees chart topper of 1979 (7)
16 Family car with an extended rear (6)
19 Scotch (6)
21 Largely frozen Russian territory (7)
23 Villainous fellow (9)
25 Edward - - -, composer of Enigma Variations (5)
27 Grip tightly (5)
28 Drew in magnetically (9)
29 Work done outside one's contracted period (8)
30 Daze, trance (6)

DOWN
1   Within reasonable limits (8)
2   Add up (5)
3   Exhaustion (9)
5   Consequence (7)
6   Edible internal parts of an animal (5)
7   Massacre (9)
8   Pinpoint (6)
9   Island in the English Channel (6)
15 Goddess of love (9)
17 Condiment (5, 4)
18 Breed of retriever (8)
20 Sail support on a ship (7)
21 Military greeting (6)
22 Hitchcock thriller (6)
24 Interval between dusk and dawn (5)
26 Arise from bed (3, 2)

Puzzles

ACROSS

1 Male head of upmarket gallery to change (6)
4 Huge waste in fuel (8)
10 Hygienic liquid to discourage man (9)
11 Currency managed in foreign country, initially (5)
12 Made a judgment describing writing paper, perhaps (5)
13 Notice easily portable theatrical lamp (9)
14 Attempt to suppress old calamity (7)
16 Residential development from eastern region of the US (6)
19 Kitchen utensil beginning to yield drink (6)
21 Southern Mediterranean peninsula is an area belonging to Russia (7)
23 Terrible cons lured rascal (9)
25 The Spanish brought back piece of jazzy music for composer (5)
27 Hold 150 in grams (5)
28 Tart cadet cooked was enticing (9)
29 In plain view, I'm on last of the extra hours (8)
30 Interminable story holds up drunkenness? (6)

DOWN

1 Fashion to assess is average (8)
2 Entire measure of rum: a litre (5)
3 Fatigue – it arises, accompanied by bloodshot appearance? (9)
5 Show up after away result (7)
6 For example, tripe is no longer fresh and all unfinished (5)
7 Small response to a joke that's killing everyone (9)
8 Find half of loaf before 100 consumed (6)
9 Cow making a jumper (6)
15 Greek deity atrophied badly (9)
17 Somehow baste all on time to make seasoning (5, 4)
18 Left a supporter to carry out Rex the dog (8)
20 Three feet and a limb in part of ship's rigging (7)
21 Show respect towards South African instrument (6)
22 Tipsy choir hides violent criminal? (6)
24 Chivalrous type mentioned period of darkness (5)
26 Clothes stand (3, 2)

Sudoku

Fill in the squares in the grid so that every row, column and each of the nine 3x3 squares contain all the digits from one to nine.

MEDIUM GRID

1	9		7	5	2			
					3			2
						6	7	
						1	6	
	1		4	7	5		3	
	2	8						
	3	7						
2			6					
			9	3	7		2	4

HARD GRID

1			3		5			4
	4		1		8		2	
7								8
		2	8		9	6		
	6						5	
		1	7		6	4		
8								9
	3		4		1		8	
9			5		7			3

Were you right? Turn to page 182 for the answers

Climb every

Harry's sons believe they've come up with a great idea for his

Words Peter Jennings / Illustration Kate Davies

Clive stood by a small tarn, looking up at the trail that disappeared into the high crag. He said: "We've come the wrong way."

His father, Harry, was unconcerned: "No matter. We'll head up there."

"To the top?"

"Where else?"

Clive's brother, Tim, was seated on a rocky outcrop with his son, Darren. They were nibbling Kendal mint cake and nodded agreement with Clive. They should return to the hotel where there was a welcoming bar. But Harry was having none of it. "We've come all this way to climb this mountain and that's what we're going to do."

Three months earlier, the brothers had met to discuss this excursion. Although they were not normally a close family, they needed to decide what to do about Harry's birthday. Seventy is a milestone, they agreed, but how to celebrate? Harry was no couch potato. His face had a rugged outdoor appearance and his legs were still firmly muscled.

It was agreed that they would take him to Cumbria to climb a mountain. And Darren, his 14-year-old grandson, would come, too.

On their journey up the M6, the rain had almost deflated their enthusiasm, but when they reached the oak-beamed hotel an excellent dinner and cheery atmosphere in the bar soon revived their spirits. The landlord assured them that the forecast for the next day was fine.

At the nearby table, sipping white wine, were a jolly woman of around Harry's age and her daughter. Stylishly dressed, they were clearly not in the Lake District to go hiking. Harry struck up a conversation and the older woman introduced herself as Julia; her daughter was called Carrie. Harry pushed the two tables together and ordered more Chardonnay for his new friends.

"You walkers are all the same," Julia teased. "Drinking and climbing; that's all you think about."

"Not all," Harry winked, and proceeded to entertain her with a fund of reminiscences. When he and Julia discovered they had been sitting not a 100 yards apart at the Isle of Wight rock festival in 1970, the rest of the party smiled politely, made their excuses and retired for the night.

In the morning, the men ate a hearty breakfast before loading their backpacks with sandwiches and anoraks. While they were putting on their walking boots, Julia and Carrie came down the stairs. "Nice to see some folks up and about early," Julia joked.

"Some folks are happier in the fresh air than lazing in bed," grinned Harry.

Julia laughed heartily and Carrie blushed. Julia said: "My daughter thinks that old people should be seen and not heard."

Harry opened the front door and pointed to the skyline. He said: "You should see the view from that hilltop. Wonderful. Take Carrie up there today - it's not a difficult climb."

Julia gave him a merry look as they went in to the restaurant. Clive looked over at his father, saying drily: "When you're ready, Dad," and the four of them set out along the lane. Darren ran ahead while the other three followed more slowly.

Harry had read the Wainwright guide and, after a mile, said: "We turn right here." Several experienced-looking walkers were striding ahead along the more obvious route. Tim and Clive exchanged doubtful glances, but followed their father up a narrow trail. It wasn't until they reached the tarn that Harry secretly doubted his own wisdom. There was not another climber in sight.

"Are we lost?" Darren asked hopefully, keen for an adventure.

"Not at all," said Harry. And he strode off up the muddy trail, hiding his apprehension.

It wasn't until they reached the tarn that Harry secretly doubted his own wisdom. There was not another climber in sight

---

The path took them over a tumbling beck. The stepping stones were slippery under their boots. They scrambled along until they came to a steep slope of loose, grey stones. Harry stood, arms folded, frowning at the challenge. Tim whispered to Clive: "He'll never make it."

Darren leapt forward, skipping from stone to stone, sending showers of pebbles cascading

mountain

birthday celebration

down. He climbed up until he appeared no larger than an ant to the observers below.

"Come on. We can't let him beat us," Harry said, starting to climb. His sons breathed deeply and followed. It took nearly an hour to catch up with Darren, who pointed to the summit, saying: "Not far now."

It was no more than a hundred yards up a steep track and soon they stood on the peak. They had conquered it! The men laughed and hugged, feeling closer as a family than they had for a long time.

Back at the hotel, they enjoyed roast lamb with a bottle of red wine before moving to the lounge for coffee. They were happily discussing the day's adventure when Julia and Carrie burst in. "We've been up a mountain!" Julia announced breathlessly.

"Actually, it was only a hill - the one you suggested," Carrie explained, more calmly.

There were loud cheers and Tim asked: "First time?"

"Yes," said Julia. "And next time I'll wear proper boots!"

The women sat down and Clive told them their climb was to celebrate Harry's birthday, adding: "We felt this might be his last trip to the Lakes."

"Nonsense," interrupted Harry. "This is the best birthday I've ever had - but not the last. Next year, Ben Nevis!"

Julia said: "So you won't be returning here then?"

Meeting her gaze, Harry asked: "Is that an invitation?"

As they were preparing to leave the next day, Clive and Tim found their father deep in conversation with Julia. After exchanging goodbyes, Tim asked him: "What was all that about?"

"None of your business!" Harry grinned, but couldn't resist adding: "If you must know, Julia was telling me she lives near the Peak District. Fine walking country, that."

Beehives and

Writer Valery McConnell and **Yours** *readers remember the hairstyles that launched a thousand snips*

Just as much as clothes, a hairstyle can announce to the world that you've grown-up and want to be taken seriously. That it's you - not your mum - who is now in charge. That first happened for me with a feather cut, aged 14. Remember those? Very layered hair - preferably fine-styled with a razor - as sported by Suzi Quatro and the girls from the New Seekers. Even better, a new, unisex hairdresser had opened up in town. No chance of your mum going there for a shampoo and set - so it was where we all got our identical cuts.

There was only one problem... we were still at school, where tied-back hair was an iron rule, so ended up sporting an unflattering rat's tail beneath layers clamped in kirby grips.

Allyson Curtis would sympathise... "In 1973 I decided, two days before I was due to begin work as a 17-year-old cadet nurse, to home-style my hair à la David Bowie. On duty I was required to tie my hair back and, as cadet nurses didn't wear caps, the look I achieved was akin to Mr Hedgehog in nurse's uniform".

It should have worked out better for independent-minded **Heather Moulson**... "Everyone else was sporting feather cuts that autumn of 1971, but I wanted the glamour of a perm. It was the overpowering smell of ammonia I remember most during that gruelling, three-hour session. The smell stayed with me for weeks. Meanwhile, I resembled a poodle being groomed for Crufts. I couldn't get a brush or comb through my hair. All the girls at school laughed at me. It was truly traumatic."

Perms! So many of you got in touch with total recall of the smell, the singe and the resulting unspeakable frizz. Yes, perms have been traumatising **Yours** readers for many years. "In 1950 I begged my

mum to let me have a perm," writes **Janet Taylor**. "The machine for the perm was a massive thing with long wires and on the end of each wire was a big metal clip which they attached to each roll of hair. The girl fixed the clip and then left me in a cubicle with curtains round. After a while the clip near my neck started burning my skin; I was in agony but kept quiet. The next day I had a massive blister across my neck and I didn't have another perm for years."

Helen Gale however, begs to differ. "I loved my shaggy perm. It was such low maintenance. Just a visit every few months for a trim and a perm, then I could wash and leave it. I have never had another hairstyle that was as easy to care for."

Which you could never say about beehives. **Wendy Lucey** recalls, with admiration, her friend's perfect up-do. "Her sister was a hairdresser and she'd drive a 40-mile round trip to style it for her. She slept with a rolled towel under her neck so the shape stayed in place and she didn't comb it from one Saturday to the next. But her hair never looked untidy as there was so much lacquer on it, I don't think it would have

Sheila Murphy: Here I am on the left with my sister-in-law, sporting Farrah Fawcett Majors flicks. It was my favourite style and I think we look quite chic.

feather cuts

Helen Gale on her wedding day in 1981, sporting her beloved shaggy perm.

Dorothy Bloor: This is my sister Gladys and me in 1959, just after we had been to the hairdressers to have Marcel Waves set in our hair – which had come back into fashion just then. We thought we were very glamorous young ladies.

moved in a force ten gale."

Yep - you have to commit to a beehive. "In 1960 when I was 16 I plagued my mother to let me have a beehive hair-do," remembers **Glennys Wood**. "She was reluctant as I had naturally curly hair. Anyway, she gave in and off I went to quite a posh, expensive salon in Derby town centre. On my way home on the bus I kept looking at my reflection, hair straightened and piled high. It looked awful! As soon as I arrived home I covered my hair in Nivea cream to flatten it down. When my mother arrived home from work she said, 'Let's have a look then'. I had made such a mess of it I had to have it washed out. I never had a beehive again."

At least Glennys could just wash the mistake away, unlike poor **Mrs Ball**. "I had beautiful waist-length hair and decided to get my highlights done at home by a supposedly professional hairdresser. She put the bleach on my hair and all seemed to go well. Eventually I leant over the bath to wash the bleach out. I looked down and there was my waist-length hair lying in the bath. She had left the bleach on too long. It was awful. I cried for days and sadly my hair would never grow that long again."

Rosemary Lake was a big Helen Shapiro fan and her friend was a trainee hairdresser, so how would that turn out? "I agreed to let her cut short and style my long, thick dark hair and she wouldn't let me look until it was finished. She had given me Helen's backcombed bob and I was delighted. I'm now 69 and I've had many different styles, but I will never forget how great that felt back in 1962." Yay!

Something

Vicky is too fond of Elsa to turn down her offer, but will it rui...

Elsa said: "Not long now, Vicky." Her young neighbour smiled back happily: "I can't believe I'll be married in a fortnight!"

"Are you all prepared for your big day?" Elsa asked.

"Everything but the dress – I pick that up next week." Vicky's face glowed – the beautiful satin gown was her one extravagance in the low-budget wedding she and Callum had planned.

Elsa smiled. Despite the 55-year age difference, she had grown very fond of Vicky since, aged 13, she had thrown a Frisbee over the fence and ruined Elsa's tulips. The next day Vicky had called round with a contrite face, and had been calling round ever since. Over the years, she had become the granddaughter that Elsa never had.

Now she glanced over at the framed photo of her own wedding. Jack had looked so smart, bless him! She chuckled: "Look at that white suit Jack wore when we got married. They were all the rage in the Sixties. He thought he was the bee's knees!"

Vicky giggled: "The flares are amazing! And your dress is lovely, Elsa."

"I've still got it. I was a trim little thing then – about your size. Why don't you try it on? It's a long time since I could fit into it."

"Go on, then," Vicky laughed.

Five minutes later, she was clad in a white dress made up of huge crocheted circles the size of dinner plates.

"Fits perfectly!" Elsa enthused. "Very different from your wedding dress, I dare say."

"It certainly is," agreed Vicky, thinking of the glamorous strapless creation waiting for her in the shop, before adding tactfully, "but this is so... so retro! Vintage gear is all the rage now."

Elsa sighed as she put the dress away. It had brought the memories flooding back and she hoped Vicky would be as radiantly happy as she had been on her big day.

However, a few days later Vicky was far from radiant. When she called round, her usual sparkle was missing.

"Vicky, dear, is something wrong?"

"No, I'm fine," Vicky said, then burst into tears.

"Sit down and tell me what's happened," Elsa urged.

Between sniffs, Vicky explained that she had gone to collect her wedding dress only to find the shop closed with a sign announcing it had gone out of business. She said: "There was a phone number to call but when I rang they just said it's under administration so I can't have the dress I ordered!"

"Oh, my poor love!"

Vicky managed a watery smile. "I should get the money back eventually, but I won't have the dress..."

An idea came to Elsa. "You can wear mine! It's a perfect fit, and you liked it, didn't you?"

"Well – yes – but it's yours," Vicky stammered. "I couldn't possibly!"

Elsa patted her hand. "Of course you could. Take it home tonight. No, don't say a word. That's settled."

That evening, Vicky's mum Janet exclaimed: "Well, isn't that kind! A vintage wedding dress. Problem solved."

In answer, Vicky silently drew the dress from its layers of tissue and held it up to the light.

"Oh," said Janet, "How – um – unusual..."

"Mum, it looks like a tablecloth."

"It might look different on."

"It does," groaned Vicky. "It ooks worse! The

Elsa sighed as she put the dress away. It had brought the memories flooding back and she hoped Vicky would be as radiantly happy as she had been on her big day

trouble is I told Elsa I loved it, but I was only trying to be nice."

Callum put his head round the door, then quickly shielded his eyes. "Whoops! I'm not meant to see the dress, am I?"

"It's okay, come in."

Callum looked puzzled. "That's not the one you chose, is it?"

Words Catherine Laybourn / Illustration Katie Wood

borrowed

her Big Day?

but, as she told her mother: "If I don't wear Elsa's dress, she'll be so hurt..."

"I'll have a word with her - see what can be done," Janet offered and went next door for a cup of tea and a chat with Elsa.

"I'm so looking forward to seeing Vicky in my dress!" Elsa told her. "I could tell she loved it."

"Well..." Janet hesitated.

"She doesn't mind it being a hand-me-down, does she?"

"Oh no - it's just that she'd set her heart on..."

Elsa studied Janet's face and said quietly: "Ah! She was just being polite, wasn't she?"

"Well, styles have changed so much," Janet mumbled, searching for an excuse.

"Don't I know it, dear. I've a wardrobe full of fashions that won't see the light of day again. None of it fits me anymore."

"Have you?" said Janet. "I'd love to have a look, if I may. I've had a thought."

On the big day, Vicky was quiet and nervous as her father drove them to the church. "Was this a bad idea, Mum?"

"No of course not," Janet said, sounding more confident than she felt.

The car pulled up in front of the assembled wedding guests and Vicky gasped in astonishment. Her friend Clare was dressed in a psychedelic kaftan and her cousin, Tina, wore a Biba mini dress with white knee-length boots.

Auntie Lou sported a knitted trouser suit while Uncle Frank wore the widest flares she'd ever seen. Vicky's boss was unrecognisable in a paisley shirt and purple velvet trousers.

Clare hugged her, saying: "Sixties fancy dress is a brilliant theme for a wedding!"

"You're the belle of the ball," Elsa told her fondly.

"Thank you, Elsa," Vicky said and kissed her.

Clutching her small posy of flowers, Vicky walked up the aisle to where Callum was waiting anxiously.

He whispered: "Do I look daft in this white suit?"

Vicky's mouth twitched with amusement. "Never! Anyway, I'd marry you even if you were wearing a bin liner!"

Vicky told him the full story of the bankrupt shop and Elsa's generous offer.

"Well, why not wear the old lady's dress?" Callum asked.

Vicky stared at him in disbelief. "But look at it!"

"Listen, love, it's you I'm marrying, not the dress. The wedding is just one day; it's all the days after that count."

"But I want to look beautiful for you!"

He smiled: "I'd marry you if you were dressed in a bin liner."

As the big day drew closer, Vicky half-heartedly scoured the charity shops for a second-hand dress

Two-speed crossword

For this puzzle we've provided two sets of clues, each giving the same answers. Quick clues are below and Cryptic to the right. It's a good way to hone your skills, because it gives you two ways to crack the crossword!

ACROSS
8 Dashingly attractive (8)
9 Undo (a knot) (5)
10 Sicilian volcano (4)
11 Phantom (5)
12 Conservative (4)
13 Position of a vendor's stall (5)
14 Leave out in the cold (9)
16 Whiff (5)
17 Picture painted on a wall (5)
22 Disco (9)
24 Persistently pursue (5)
26 Ray of light (4)
27 Local constable? (5)
28 Vegetable of the onion family (4)
29 Sorcery (5)
30 From our continent (8)

DOWN
1 Skipper (7)
2 Went ahead (8)
3 Stuff (oneself) with food (5)
4 Sorrow caused by guilt (7)
5 Small yellow flower (9)
6 Motionless (6)
7 Subjugate (7)
15 The - - - of Notre-Dame, classic novel by Victor Hugo (9)
18 Animal such as a gazelle or gnu (8)
19 Awkward problem (7)
20 Acrobat (7)
21 Unlawful (7)
23 Respect paid to another (6)
25 Tight stretchy fabric (5)

Puzzles

ACROSS

8 Pass a few looking good (8)
9 Disentangle from the Beeb after it loses capital (5)
10 Peak in Italy and in France and North America (4)
11 Good TV presenter – one might be seen on Most Haunted Live, perhaps (5)
12 Politician is a part of history (4)
13 What cricketers play on asphalt? (5)
14 Socially exclude one taken in by Socrates, oddly (9)
16 Smell nothing grim (5)
17 It's what happens when an artist goes to the wall! (5)
22 Entertainment venue for chivalrous group, we hear (9)
24 Follow small lecture (5)
26 Where you might see a gymnast smile broadly (4)
27 Ball, perhaps, for a policeman (5)
28 Heard to disclose Welsh symbol (4)
29 Mother and soldier caught conjuring tricks (5)
30 German or Spaniard? A pure one, possibly (8)

DOWN

1 Biblical killer devouring appropriate army officer (7)
2 A jig with 500 gets very complex (8)
3 Any one of six kings relinquishes English ravine (5)
4 Regret about code (7)
5 Insert carbon into flatter plant (9)
6 Still crackling with electricity? (6)
7 Keep in check to produce more records, perhaps (7)
15 Gut feeling to put a bet on fellow with a stoop (9)
18 Worker to run off and marry a beast! (8)
19 Detective Inspector left Austen heroine a tough choice (7)
20 Glass mechanism in a lock (7)
21 Harm, for example, a learner outside of the law (7)
23 Tribute period after queen receives ring (6)
25 Some really crazy material (5)

Sudoku

Fill in the squares in the grid so that every row, column and each of the nine 3x3 squares contain all the digits from one to nine.

MEDIUM GRID

			8					
4	5				2			
2						7		5	8
						2		4
5		3		4		9		6
	8		9					
9	4		3					7
				6			3	4
					1			

HARD GRID

		5	9		6		
7				3				4
	1						9	
			1			8	
	4		6		5		1
		9			2		
	7						6
6				7				2
			3		8	7	

Were you right? Turn to page 182 for the answers

Blind date

Chloe isn't looking for love, but her friend Sienna is...

Words Lesley Spencer / Illustration Kate Davies

On Thursday morning, my glamorous friend Sienna dropped me at our local hospital before going to park her car. I made my way to the crowded coffee bar, waving to Grace, a fellow volunteer who was near the entrance wearing her Ask Me for Help badge.

Normally the coffee bar is quiet, just a few tables of people huddled over their prescriptions. "What's going on?" I asked Grace.

"Blood drive," she replied. "These are all donors recovering with a cup of tea."

No hope of privacy, I thought. I was here as a 'wingman' for Sienna, who was having her first date with a man she'd contacted through a dating agency. Not really my kind of thing, although I admired her adventurous spirit. The thought of dating again in my 50s scared me to death.

The previous week, Sienna had called me on my mobile as I walked my Scottish terrier, Bouncy. A sense of unease gripped me, as it always does when Sienna mentions men.

"You need to branch out, Chloe," she'd said. "Your Dave was a treasure, but it's been five years now."

"I'm fine. If there's someone out there for me, we'll find each other."

"Be more proactive. Guess what I've done?"

"Dyed your hair red?" I asked. "Moved into a gypsy caravan?"

"I've signed up with the Puppy Love dating agency. It's for people who share a love of animals."

Sienna works at an animal sanctuary. Bouncy had been one of its rescue dogs. Any man suited to Sienna would have to like animals, so maybe this Puppy Love thing was a good idea.

"They've found me a match," she announced. "And I need your help. I'm arranging a first date with Pete604."

"He's got a number? Is he in prison?"

"That's his dating agency number. I'm Melissa200."

"But your name isn't Melissa."

"And his probably isn't Pete."

"I see," I replied, although I didn't.

"I have to choose a safe location for the first date. Somewhere public where he can't attack me with a chainsaw."

I privately felt it would be a brave man who tackled Sienna with any implement.

"I've decided on the coffee bar at the hospital; you can sit on the other side of the room, making sure nothing bad happens."

So here I was. I bought a latte and found a table with three other people. The man next to me scraped his chair closer to the wall to make room. I thanked him. He was about my age, tall and thin, with glasses.

I scanned the room for Sienna or a man who might be Pete604. A thought struck me. Perhaps Sienna's date was the man next to me? He saw me studying him and our eyes met.

"I don't mean to be rude," I said, "but is your name Pete?" I didn't add the 604 bit.

"My name's Michael," he said. "Yours?"

"Chloe. Sorry. I mistook you for someone else."

I went back to studying the room. It occurred to me that maybe his real name was Michael, but in the dating agency he was Pete. I took another discreet look. He was reading some kind of technical manual. I glanced away quickly before he sensed my gaze.

She was sitting opposite a burly man with thinning hair. I couldn't hear their words, but I watched the body language

---

Then I spotted Sienna. She was sitting opposite a burly man with thinning hair. I couldn't hear their words, but I watched the body language. Sienna brushed back her hair; Pete brushed his back. Sienna stirred her coffee; Pete stirred his. I stirred my coffee, watching that Pete didn't pull out a chainsaw.

"Excuse me," said a soft voice beside me.

"Yes?"

"You're stirring my tea."

I looked down - I'd put sugar in his cup and was

stirring it.

"Sorry!" I said. "I was distracted. Would you like another one?"

"This is fine."

I looked back at Sienna and Pete. Things didn't seem to be going well.

Sienna leaned forward. Pete leaned forward. Then they both sat back with their hands on their knees.

"Chloe?" It was the man beside me again.

"Yes... Michael?"

"You have your hand on my knee."

I was shocked to find he was right. My fingers were curled on the soft twill of his trousers. I removed my hand swiftly.

"This table is very small."

"I'm not really complaining..."

"I'm so sorry."

"Don't apologise."

I noticed he was wearing a volunteer badge. I leaned closer to read it. "I work with the hospital radio," he said.

"I'm in the pharmacy." I unbuttoned my jacket to reveal my badge. "My friend is on a blind date with a man over there, and I'm supposed to watch in case he turns out to be violent."

Michael peered across. "I've seen him before," he said. "He gave a talk on our radio. He's a retired police officer."

"I hope he likes animals," I reflected out loud.

Michael smiled. "I have two cats. They're welcome company since I've been... on my own."

I looked at him properly for the first time and noticed the attractive crinkles around his eyes. I liked the fact that he was wearing a cardigan that someone who loved him had clearly knitted. The crowded room, filled with chatter, receded. I suddenly knew this man was special. I forced myself to breathe deeply while praying that he liked cuddly women and Scottish terriers.

Sienna was pushing her way towards me, bumping into chairs and making the china rattle. "No good," she whispered. "Couldn't get a word in edgeways. Too used to barking commands."

Should I tell her about Michael who liked animals and had two cats? No, I decided I wanted this man for myself. Ignoring Sienna, Michael turned to me: "I'm on my way to give blood. Would you like to come with me?"

"I certainly would."

So our first date was to a blood bank. What would the Puppy Love dating agency have made of that?

SUN GLASSES 1/- PER PAIR
QUALITY LIDO LENSES

Pass the

Writer Valery McConnell and **Yours** *readers remember rain, wind and soggy sausage rolls. Yes, you've guessed, it must be a holiday in Britain!*

If you're over 50, you'll have a holiday memory of being determined to enjoy yourself whatever the weather. Mine is the cold, wet week in the South of Ireland – me, my sister, Mum and Dad, Granny and Granda, all crammed into Granda's Ford Popular, with a travelling rug for warmth. It didn't stop us picnicking – huddled beside the Primus stove in our Pac-a-Macs eating sausages and drinking strong tea while a gale blew around us.

Susan Smith has similar memories – except she was squeezed into her granddad's Hillman…"There were three adults in the back with my sister, Gillian, and in the front would be Granddad, Dad and me – with me sitting on a cushion on the handbrake. We were going to Skegness, where we stayed at

Mrs Groocock's boarding house. In those days you left the B&B after breakfast and couldn't go back until nearly tea time. We would go to the beach and one day I remember, it started to rain heavily but, as we had paid for deckchairs and windbreaks, we sat on the beach with our raincoats and umbrellas even though we were the only ones there. We spent many a happy hour on the beach in the pouring rain." I think that last sentence sums up the British holiday spirit.

I'm sure **Margaret Simpson** would agree. She recalls: "One memorable Spring Bank Holiday in the early Seventies we took our small caravan and two little boys to a lovely site in the Yorkshire Dales, where it proceeded to pour down for at least 36 hours. This resulted in both boys sailing their boats in the huge puddle which had formed around the caravan steps."

But at least you are dry inside a caravan. Unlike those under canvas…

Remember Carry On Camping? Well, **Mrs Jones** could have written the script… "We set off to the Aberystwyth area on a lovely, sunny day and erected the tent on raised ground near a river. As I unpacked, I realised we'd left our clothes behind, apart from underwear and t-shirts. Then the rains came down and the river burst its banks. Although we survived, people were flooded out and we couldn't settle in the commotion. Early next morning we packed up our van, which, of course, was now stuck fast in the mud. I gave the back end a shove and the back wheels spun and my only clothing – a light-coloured tracksuit – was plastered in thick mud."

Camping holidays are not for softies… "I remember packing our wet camping gear on top of the car and the doors wouldn't shut," writes **Pat Berkshire**. "The weight of the soaked tent caused the car roof to sag. We had to unpack everything and dry it out before we could go home. We bought a trailer for the next trip!"

In 1945, Londoner **Doreen Paganini**, with her mum and gran, had gone to visit her evacuated Aunty Rose and family in Bolton. "It was decided to take us kids to Blackpool. We

Cooling off at the lido… but the weather wasn't always so sunny.

Pac-a-Mac...

PIC: ALAMY

FREE
BOOKLET
Send P.C. to
BUTLIN'S LTD.
(Dept. H.B.)
439, OXFORD ST
LONDON, W.1.

From holiday camps to Carry On Camping… the great British summer was often bracing!

were so excited to be going to the seaside, we could hardly contain ourselves as we set off to the railway station.

"The first disaster was when Rose stepped on to the train and her shoe fell off on to the line. The station attendant said there was nothing that could be done until the train had left the station. So while the rest of us went to Blackpool, Rose and baby Freddy waited to retrieve her shoe. On our arrival, we simply sat and waited for our relatives and eventually their train pulled in. Hurrah, all was well. Except as we finally walked out of the station,

the heavens opened and it didn't seem as though it was ever going to stop. It didn't.

"We couldn't see any cafés or shops, except, just outside the station, a stall with a small canopy. None of us managed to get under the canopy, but we stood there in the rain eating pork pies and sausage rolls, while we waited for the next train to arrive to go back to Bolton. Fortunately, it wasn't too long after our disastrous day out that we were all back in our own homes in London waiting for VE Day."

At least Doreen and co were

upholding the great British tradition of picnicking in the rain.

After all, the best thing about a weather-beaten British seaside holiday is having a great tale to tell afterwards. And I think **Margaret Anderson's** takes the biscuit.

"Some years ago my father had booked a coach trip to Bournemouth on Easter Monday for himself, me and my four-year-old, Sam. As all my son wanted to do was dig in the sand, we took a bucket and spade. On arriving in Bournemouth it had just started to snow! But so as not to disappoint my son, we sat on the sand under the pier with snow falling each side of us.

"Incidentally, we were not the only ones to have a happy time that day - even if we were a little mad!"

We'll meet

Every soldier needs a girl to come home to...

Jack Saunders and his son Ted were engrossed in their weekly ritual - only this time it was different. This time they were planning the last performance of The Saunders Syncopaters.

Ted had received his call up papers. Ronnie, their drummer, had already gone and Jimmy, their vocalist, was expecting his call to serve King and country any day now.

Jack cast a critical eye over the list: "So, you're startin' with That's A-plenty. Good. Then The Indian Love Call - always goes down well, does that. A couple of Al Bowlly numbers. Now then, what about your slow numbers?"

"Well, I was thinking Smoke Gets In Your Eyes and As Time Goes By," said Ted.

"Watch that middle eight in Smoke, you made a right dog's breakfast of that last time."

Ted smiled tolerantly; ever since his dad had taught him the clarinet as a boy he'd kept a close eye on his musical career. Jack carried on down the list, nodding approval, until he reached the closing number. "What's this? I Love You Truly to finish? For God's sake, lad, this is the last time you'll be playin' together. You need summat to send 'em 'ome 'appy. 'Ow about Wish Me Luck As You Wave Me Goodbye?"

Ted shook his head. "No, Dad, I'm settled on that one."

"What are you thinkin' of? You never finish with a soft tune like that. You'll send 'em to sleep!"

"Dad, I'm having it."

"Well, 'ave it your own way, but it wouldn't be my choice."

Jack stomped out of the room. Ted lit a cigarette and watched the smoke float in the air. His father meant well, but it had to be that song. He had it all planned. It would be his message to Jeanne.

Pretty, smiling Jeanne, with her blue eyes and chestnut hair. He'd spotted her from the stage the first night she came dancing with her friend Hilda. She shone out among all the other girls. He wasted no time in finding out her name, but could never summon up the nerve to talk to her apart from a few shy words at the bar.

He watched for her at every dance, praying she wouldn't turn up with a young man. Ted wished he had plenty of time to court her, but the war made everything uncertain. He knocked the ash decisively from his cigarette. He had to let her know how he felt. If a man was going into the army, he needed a girl back home, someone to fight for, a girl to come back to.

His plan was to send her a note telling her to listen out for the last song of the evening, then he'd get Jimmy to announce it was for a special girl. His only worry was that she might not turn up.

On Saturday night he arrived at the hall to find that his father had put a banner over the stage wishing him good luck. He knew it was going to be hard on his parents. Tenderly, Ted lifted his precious clarinet from its case.

Jimmy arrived and slapped him on the back. "Well, this is it, old son, last time. Let's do 'em proud, eh? Now what about this note for the lovely Jeanne?" Ted handed him the scrap of paper. "Leave it to me," Jimmy grinned, putting the note in his top pocket and patting it.

As the night wore on, Ted watched anxiously until he spotted Jeanne amid the swirling couples. He saw his

---

She shone out among all the other girls. He wasted no time in finding out her name, but could never summon up the nerve to talk to her apart from a few shy words at the bar

---

parents arrive, creeping in quietly at the back.

Jimmy appeared with two pints of mild. "Don't worry about your 'Jeannie with the light brown hair', I'll do such a good job of that number she'll be all over you!" Ted thumped his friend on the arm, hoping he was right.

Words Maddie Purslow / Illustration Katie Wood

again

As the last number approached, Ted felt sick with nerves. Jimmy stepped up to the mike and said: "This song is for a very special girl" - but before a note had passed his lips, Jack jumped up on to the stage, waving his hands for silence.

"Sorry, Jimmy lad, you've a grand voice, but I've summat to say." The room stood still, all eyes on him. "Ladies and gentlemen, as you may know, this is the last time the band will be playing together. My son, Ted, is leaving to fight for his country and make us all proud. I think you'll all agree, he needs a proper send off!"

The room erupted into applause. Jack began to sing the opening words of Good-bye-ee and the audience joined in. Ted saw his mother weeping in the front row.

As the band packed away, he felt hollow inside. He'd missed his chance, thanks to his well-meaning father. Just then, one of the hall doors creaked open and Jeanne crept quietly in. Shyly, she approached the stage.

"Hello, Ted."

"Hello," he said, hardly daring to look at her.

"I think that was wonderful what your dad did for you, just now." Ted nodded agreement.

"I, um, got your note," said Jeanne. "I know it didn't go how you planned. Jimmy told me."

Ted remained dumb, wishing he had Jimmy's easy confidence around girls.

"Well, anyway," Jeanne went on, "I've got something for you." From behind her back she produced a roll of paper. "It's sheet music. When I knew you were going, I got Mr Atkins at the music shop to order it in, special."

She handed it to Ted. "It's me favourite, is that, and I thought if you play it while you're away, it might make you think of me, back home. Go on - open it!"

Slowly, Ted unfurled the paper. His heart jumped for joy when he read the title: I Love You Truly.

Stretching up, Jeanne kissed him gently on the cheek.

Two-speed crossword

For this puzzle we've provided two sets of clues, each giving the same answers. Quick clues are below and Cryptic to the right. It's a good way to hone your skills, because it gives you two ways to crack the crossword!

ACROSS
3 Presenter who often broadcasts before the 4D (10)
8 Himalayan tongue (6)
9 Scaremonger (8)
10 Brief overview (8)
11 Blocked against entry (6)
12 Held tightly, cuddled (8)
15 Mainstream, having wide general appeal (6-2-3-4)
17 Writer of music (8)
19 Sewing implement (6)
23 Mountain transport (5, 3)
24 Island on which the city of Hobart is located (8)
25 Staggered and swayed (6)
26 Establishes (10)

DOWN
1 Canine's shelter (6)
2 - - - grass, tall ornamental plant (6)
3 Woman's garment worn in bed (10)
4 Meteorological prediction (7, 8)
5 Suddenly stand on hind legs (4)
6 Part of a three-piece suite? (8)
7 Guarantee (6)
11 Publication for children such as The Beano (5)
13 Locked in jail (6, 4)
14 Sidestep (5)
16 Politician who negotiates with other nations (8)
18 Acquire (6)
20 Prime number (6)
21 Foliage (6)
22 Dark spot in timber (4)

Puzzles

ACROSS

3 Huw Edwards, say, answered badly about religious education (10)
8 Asian language I write backwards to trap a learner (6)
9 Little Albert, a Royal Marine, is initially the one who spreads panic (8)
10 Damages stolen photograph (8)
11 Shut near beginning of dusk (6)
12 Hugged English managing director bagging a pair of pheasants? (8)
15 Banal place for a traffic island? (6-2-3-4)
17 For instance, Bach or Beethoven mostly come with baffling problem (8)
19 Require the French to cause irritation (6)
23 Taxi left race, returning for a different mode of transport (5, 3)
24 Reservists' enthusiasm for Australian state (8)
25 Embarrassed about slender fish brought in by fisherman (6)
26 Centres of research test in situ, possibly (10)

DOWN

1 Know either side of nice large doghouse (6)
2 Motorway goes through father's plains (6)
3 Red things tailored with small item of sleepwear (10)
4 Orchestrate a few changes for a report on future conditions (7, 8)
5 Raise the back section (4)
6 Prepare to fight head of meeting for seat (8)
7 Make certain headless chickens rue blunders (6)
11 Company: one invested in compère and funny man (5)
13 Not keeping up with drinking places in prison (6, 4)
14 Wild West city to avoid? (5)
16 Ambassador producing certificate on time (8)
18 Broken baton I receive (6)
20 Cricket team partaking in novel event (6)
21 Abandons pages (6)
22 Some banknotes become entangled (4)

Sudoku

Fill in the squares in the grid so that every row, column and each of the nine 3x3 squares contain all the digits from one to nine.

MEDIUM GRID

4				7		6		8
		2					4	
			9					7
	7				3			
		5	8		1	4		
			7				3	
9					2			
	6						8	
3		8		6				9

HARD GRID

		6			8		7	4
				2		9		
			4		9	2		6
	7				3		4	2
	2					6		
5	6		1				3	
3		7	2		5			
	4			1				
6	9		8			5		

Were you right? Turn to page 182 for the answers

A clean sweep

Does Margaret love her Hoover more than her husband?

It was the extra mess that bothered Margaret. She'd always been houseproud. "A right worry wart," Len said. He used to say it with an affectionate smile when he was working, but now he'd retired he said it in a resigned way.

On her hands and knees dusting the skirting board, Margaret sighed. 'If only he could find a hobby', she thought. 'Anything to take him out so I can get back to my normal routine'.

The bathroom door opened and Len emerged, clutching a damp towel. But Margaret only saw steam billowing. The mirror would need cleaning again.

"What's for breakfast, love?" Len asked. "Shall I make us some bacon and eggs?"

Margaret blanched at the thought. There was the bath to scrub, the mirror to buff up and the floor to mop. She didn't need frying pans to scour as well.

"Sit down with the paper," she coaxed. "I'll make some toast - much healthier than a fry-up."

Len's crestfallen expression made Margaret feel guilty. He probably missed his work as much as she missed him working, she reflected, as she popped two slices of bread in the toaster and gave the worktop a quick wipe.

The post arrived and she found Len staring at a letter, thoughtfully. "You might be right about the toast," he said. "I had a cholesterol check last week and the doc wants to see me." A wave of fear swept over her. What if Len fell ill now? It would be so unfair!

"Ah, don't you worry, pet," Len smiled. "It'll be nothing, you'll see." He went off to phone for an appointment, leaving the newspaper all askew on the sofa and the envelope on the carpet where it had fallen.

When Len had gone, Margaret forced herself to sit down for a change and leave the housework. She'd offered to go with him, but he insisted he'd be fine. "Anyway," he teased as he grabbed his keys, "isn't it bedroom cleaning on Tuesday mornings?"

Margaret didn't do the bedroom this Tuesday. She sat on the sofa, imagining how life would be without Len: not worth living. Even though they'd lived separate lives with Len working all hours and Margaret happy to stay at home, they had always rubbed along very well together without any spats, sulks or affairs.

Margaret had looked forward to Len's retirement, envisaging days out to the coast in the car, or going to London by train, side by side in a first class carriage.

She couldn't understand Len's fascination, but as she idly glanced at one of the clues, she found she knew the answer

---

Distractedly, she picked up the paper, finding it open at the crossword page, as usual. She couldn't understand Len's fascination, but as she idly glanced at one of the clues, she found she knew the answer.

When the clock chimed, she looked up with a start. 'Goodness', she thought, 'I've been doing

Words Ginette Pooley / Illustration Kate Davies

Margaret brightened. Long walks would be perfect, taking him out from under her feet.

Len looked sheepish. "The thing is, love, I don't fancy walking on my own. I know you wouldn't want to come, with your cleaning and that, so when the doc told me Mrs Phillips had died and her dog needs rehoming..."

Margaret was horrified. 'Her dog? He wants you to have her dog!' Thoughts of muddy paws and moulting hair flashed through her mind, but she was so relieved that Len wasn't ill she agreed to a two-week trial.

Next morning, Len came in carrying a small black poodle with bright, friendly eyes. "It doesn't moult, love," he assured her. He set the dog down and immediately it trotted over to Margaret and sat squarely at her feet, looking up at her.

"What's it called?" she asked, stroking the little head, trying not to be too taken by it. "Ruby."

Ruby followed Margaret around as she worked, curling up nearby. "Shouldn't you be taking her out?" she asked, wanting to plump up the cushions.

He glanced up from his crossword. "The doc said Mrs Phillips kept Ruby's lead on the hall table and Ruby would fetch it when she needed a walk."

Margaret glanced into the hall. Len had dumped the lead on her polished mahogany! She winced but left it there, thinking she'd train Ruby to retrieve it from the coat hook instead.

After lunch, Ruby ran to fetch her lead, but it was Margaret she took it to. "Oh look, she wants you to come," Len said, eagerly.

Margaret huffed but inwardly felt a small thrill. "I'll come this once, just to get her used to you," she conceded, fetching her jacket.

Len headed across the park and up on to the downs. In 40 years of living there, Margaret had never ventured on to the downs. As Ruby bounced around Margaret stood there, taking in the glorious view and wondered why.

"I wish we'd brought a flask and a sandwich," Margaret said. Len nodded: "Good idea - and no mess to vacuum up afterwards."

Margaret was aghast. 'Am I really that bad?' she wondered. On the way home, she made a decision. "What say we take the car tomorrow, Len, and drive to the coast? We could take a picnic."

Len looked delighted, then hesitated. "But it's Thursday," he said, "isn't that kitchen day?"

"Blow the kitchen," Margaret cried, "we're retired. Let's have some fun."

She clipped on Ruby's lead and added with a wink: "Oh, and bring your newspaper - I'll help you with the crossword!"

this silly crossword and the bedroom is not even started'. She sprang to her feet - then remembered Len. Where on earth was he all this time? Something must be very wrong. Tears pricked her eyes. Slumped on the sofa, she left the bed unmade and the washing up in the sink. What was the point of anything without Len?

Half an hour later, his key turned in the lock and there he was, beaming. "The doc says I've got to change my lifestyle," he announced, waving a leaflet. "Chicken and fish with steamed veg and plenty of fruit."

Margaret breathed a sigh of relief. "And regular exercise, too. Long walks."

It wouldn't

*Writer Valery McConnell and **Yours** readers remember the things it's hard to believe we got up to as children...*

There can't be many adults over 50 who didn't go around when young pretending to puff away on sweet cigarettes before eating them. I certainly did.

Adults didn't bat an eyelid. Indeed, at my primary school my end-of-year prize was a chocolate smoker's kit – pipe, matches, tobacco and cigs. There would be uproar today. But society, and our parents, were less worried about dangerous influences back then, as **Helen Leah** can testify. "My dad and granddad smoked pipes.

"To ensure that I didn't feel left out, my family bought me a plastic red and yellow pipe so that I could pretend to smoke alongside them. I was also taught how to fill it with tobacco. I was about seven at the time. One Christmas, when I was about eight, everyone was enjoying a glass of port.

"My mother handed me a glass telling me that it was Ribena, but it was port. They all laughed as my face went through various contortions and it put me off drinking anything alcoholic until I was 25!"

And if today's parents would be horrified by such tricks being played on the young, imagine what they would make of this much-loved toy owned by **Marie Norman**. "In the early Sixties when I was about nine years old, I was given a toy cooker which used tea-light candles on the hob. I loved trying to cook sweets. Making a toy using naked flames would never be allowed now."

In fact, adults seemed to like ramming home the point that we lived in a dangerous world, so the sooner we got used to it, the better. Take **Margaret Rymer's** teachers, for instance. "When my sister and I were at primary school, we were asked to decant almost boiling water from the sink into a very large bowl, using jam jars. But, as I was stretching over my sister's arm, the very hot water caused the jar to break and the water went all over her upper arm – scalding her. She was taken to the doctor to have it dressed but, luckily, had no lasting scars." You notice Margaret doesn't even think the jagged, broken glass worth mentioning. We were tough back then.

Mrs Pearce's teachers shared the 'toughen them up' mindset, too. "When the trolley bus didn't run due to bad weather, we had to walk to school in the neighbouring town. We had to go under two railway bridges which flooded when we had rain.

"The boys would roll their trouser legs up higher and girls

Embrace the fear... playtime was one big adventure.

happen today

would tuck our hemlines up the legs of our navy-blue knicker-leg elastic. We took our shoes and socks off and then waded through the dirty smelly water which bubbled around our knees. We were reprimanded by teachers for being a few minutes late even though we had walked two miles. They said we should have got out of bed earlier."

In fact, with grown-ups like this shopkeeper around, it's a wonder some of us got to adulthood at all. "My husband, John, and his chums liked explosions and found a way of making gunpowder," said **Christine Birds**. "John would go into the chemist shop in the nearby town and ask for 8oz of saltpetre. The pharmacist would say, 'Are you making gunpowder, lad?'

"When John said he was, he still sold it to a 12 year old! John mixed it with sulphur and charcoal. Next they would go to the tip to look for a short length of old pipe, hammer one end flat and make a hole in one side. This was the 'weapon' in which they would pour some of the powder together with a ball bearing. Pointing the weapon at a tree, they would insert a lighted match into the hole and bang - they'd see how far the ball bearing had travelled. And as soon as fireworks were on sale, John and his friends would buy bangers which, one at a time, were placed in a fresh cowpat. They would light the touch paper and run for cover to watch the results - exploding cow poo!

"Once, one of the lads didn't

Health and Safety would have something to say about this… what could possibly go wrong?

move fast enough and they took him home plastered in it. His mother made him take his clothes off on the doorstep!"

Just William, eat your heart out... And I'm pleased to say it wasn't just the boys taking their lives in their hands. **Ellen Jones** grew up in North Wales in the mid-Sixties and proudly lists her dangerous activities. "1) Swinging out over a river on a single rope swing from the bank. The rope snapped, I was drenched and broke my ankle. 2) There were loads of open mineworks and, aged eight or nine, my friends and I walked across the hole on a plank of

wood. If we had fallen in, it was hundreds of feet deep. 3) A group of us went skating on a frozen lake; talk about thin ice. When my mother came looking for me, she grounded me for a week."

But the prize must go to **Jo Masters'** husband for proving that the past is indeed a different country - and we did things very differently there. She revealed: "When my husband was ten or 12 years old, he walked to school in rural Kent and took his shotgun and shot rabbits on the way, which he sold to the headmaster for half a crown each. His gun was then kept in the potting shed until home time."

Let's play ball

Ellen finds that being a modern grandma is quite a challenge

Ellen asked brightly: "Well, Christopher, what shall we do today?" The sullen child didn't look up at her, but continued to stare at the TV.

"What about the park? Your mum used to love feeding the ducks when she was little. I think I have some stale bread..." she tailed off, seeing her enthusiasm was falling on deaf ears.

"No! I hate the park!" Christopher stuffed another handful of sweets into his mouth from the bowl in front of him.

Ellen sighed. How much easier babysitting had been when he was tiny and content to lie quietly in his buggy. What was she to do with this unresponsive little boy who regarded her with such resentment?

She thought, 'Maybe it's my fault, we just haven't bonded – or whatever they call it nowadays. We should play together; it's a pity he didn't bring any toys. All he does is watch cartoons. How sad'.

Turning off the TV, she suggested: "Christopher, shall we find a jigsaw puzzle?" Christopher's mouth turned down defiantly. "I was watchin' that!"

"I know you were, but you've been watching it ever since you came and Granny wants to spend some time with you."

"Want Power Rangers!" Christopher screamed. "I hate comin' here! Want TV!" He beat his fists on the hearth

rug, sending the bowl of Smarties flying.

Ellen bit her lip. She looked across to Harry's photo on the sideboard. His eyes smiled back at her. 'Come on, old girl, you can do this! You raised our children just fine and grandchildren are no different', he seemed to say.

"Christopher, sweetheart..." Clumsily, Ellen got down on the floor beside him and stroked his hair. "Don't cry, darling. You can have it back on if you really want."

When Ellen's daughter, Susie, came to pick him up, Christopher's flushed cheeks betrayed their conflict. She asked: "Have you had a rough time, Mum? Was Chris playing up again?"

"He did get a bit upset when I turned the TV off," Ellen admitted. "I think he watches it far too much..."

"Oh, Mum! All kids watch TV." Then her face softened. "If you really can't cope with this I'll find a nursery for him."

As they left, Ellen said: "Goodbye, Christopher. See you next week."

"Don't like you," Christopher muttered.

'It's a shame, but I don't

like you much, either', Ellen thought as she shut the door. She poured herself a glass of sherry, held it up to Harry's picture in silent salute, then went to Google 'childcare' on her computer.

The next week when Susie and Christopher arrived, Ellen said: "Don't take his coat off, we're going to the park."

Susie looked doubtful, but Ellen turned to her grandson. "Look, Christopher. I have a new ball – with Power Rangers on it!"

So they kicked the ball about

'We've cracked it, Harry', Ellen thought. Never mind that her legs were killing her and her heart was beating 19 to the dozen

---

in the park – a 63 year old with a dodgy hip and a stumbling little boy who didn't know how to run or catch. "Quick! Go and get it before it rolls away!" she laughed – and soon he was laughing, too.

"Look, Gran! I'm David Beckham," he cried – and for the first time that she could remember, he smiled at her.

'We've cracked it, Harry', Ellen thought. Never mind that her legs were killing her and her heart was beating 19 to the dozen.

On the way home, Christopher told her the complicated plot of the last

Words Melanie Davis / Illustration Katie Wood

word? It must have been off the television."

Harry's eyes smiled kindly back at her, as always.

The next week, Ellen sat Christopher on a kitchen stool where he wriggled and kicked his legs. Taking a deep breath, she said: "Christopher, I owe you an apology. The other day you said a naughty word. No, not naughty, unacceptable! That made Granny cross, but she was wrong to smack you because hitting people is unacceptable, too. I'm very sorry and promise I'll never do it again."

Christopher eyed her solemnly. "Play ball now?" he asked.

Ellen glanced out of the window at the rain. "How about an indoor treasure hunt?" she said. "We could be pirates..."

"Or Power Rangers!"

A few weeks later, Susie invited Ellen to a barbecue. "Well, you and my son make a fine team," her son-in-law, Richard, told her after they had shown off their catching and throwing skills.

"He's very good, even with the really high ones," Ellen told him. "How his granddad would have enjoyed playing with him!"

Richard looked uncomfortable, as they all did when Harry was mentioned. His death was still too recent. Susie asked hastily: "Would you like a lolly now, Chris? How about a nice lemon one after all that running about?"

Christopher shook his head. "Want choc ice!" he demanded, pouting. "Lollies are... are..." he looked up sharply at Ellen before ending lamely, "rubbish." Ellen leaned over and gave him a high five. They'd got that off the TV.

Power Rangers episode. "Would you like an ice cream?" Ellen asked, flushed with triumph.

"Yeah!" They stopped at the corner shop and Ellen searched in the deep freezer.

"There's a strawberry lolly..."

"I want that one," Christopher pointed to a choc ice.

Ellen hesitated. "I think you'd be better with a lolly." Christopher's face went red, and his lip began to wobble. "That one!" he demanded.

Ellen took a deep breath, aware that other shoppers were looking at her. "No, darling.

You can't have that one." Christopher flung himself on the floor. The shopkeeper gave her a sympathetic smile, but an elderly customer looked disapproving.

"That one!" Christopher bawled. "The lollies are CRAP!"

"What did you say?" Ellen gasped - and smacked him firmly on the bottom, just as she would have done her own children.

"I failed!" she told Harry that night. "I earned his trust, but I threw it away by smacking him. I just couldn't help myself. Where did he learn that awful

Two-speed crossword

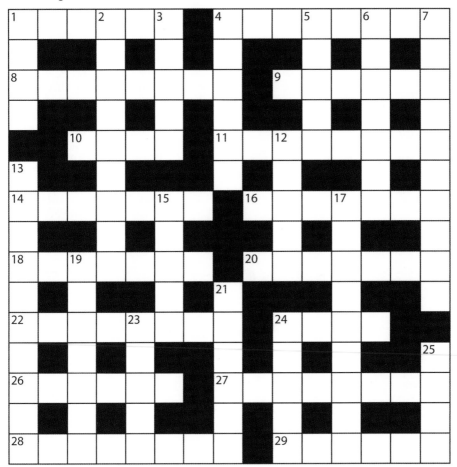

For this puzzle we've provided two sets of clues, each giving the same answers. Quick clues are below and Cryptic to the right. It's a good way to hone your skills, because it gives you two ways to crack the crossword!

ACROSS
1   Lubricant applied to machinery (6)
4   Play's artistic boss (8)
8   Emancipate, let loose (8)
9   James - - -, Hollywood icon who was known for playing gangsters (6)
10 Specific day (4)
11 Appreciative (8)
14 Cash, wonga (7)
16 Outer garments (7)
18 Business or personal interests (7)
20 Advanced university degree (7)
22 Powered by batteries or mains (8)
24 Promontory (4)
26 Rely (6)
27 Michael Jackson hit (8)
28 Woodland bird (8)
29 Capture in a snare (6)

DOWN
1   Winner's medal (4)
2   - - - Burke, 2008 winner of The X Factor (9)
3   Rub out (5)
4   Promise (6)
5   Conscript (5)
6   Cedar or pine, eg (7)
7   Top hand in poker (5, 5)
12 Dominant male in a group (5)
13 Bruce Willis science fiction disaster film (10)
15 Misjudgment (5)
17 Device for keeping a plane on course (9)
19 Shabby cinema (7)
21 Whisky (6)
23 Island kingdom east of Fiji (5)
24 Slice (roast meat) (5)
25 Object used by an actor on stage (4)

Puzzles

ACROSS

1 Musical is smooth, with Ginger Rogers initially leading (6)
4 Movie executive procured changes (8)
8 Release learner I tell off (8)
9 Lacey's detective sidekick is wary about head of narcotics (6)
10 Take out fruit (4)
11 Pleased to annoy half of Fulham (8)
14 Prepares money (7)
16 Screwed-up paper shoved inside a large outfit (7)
18 Just seconds after a female's extra-marital relations (7)
20 Address for boy's golf tournament (7)
22 Buzzing to vote for wealthy to cut back (8)
24 Close-fitting hat and English cloak (4)
26 Be sure European is ejected from part of pool (6)
27 Exciting film of personnel in control of ship (8)
28 Flap after eccentric bird (8)
29 Catch disruptive parent (6)

DOWN

1 Good old king's present? (4)
2 Unwind and relax with a former queen consort (9)
3 Delete ages on end of page (5)
4 Give a firm assurance of parking space that's high and narrow (6)
5 Plan sounds like a breeze! (5)
6 Talk with others about one that's spruce? (7)
7 Two men with lots of money – it's what card players might aim for (5, 5)
12 Final phase involves Greek character (5)
13 Cataclysmic conflict made dragon perturbed (10)
15 Lose head in state of panic, making mistake (5)
17 Car trial – it provides aid for aviation (9)
19 Dilapidated picture house is bound to slot in well (7)
21 Put an end to having crib in school (6)
23 Pacific nation partly put on games (5)
24 Cut right into hollow in the rock (5)
25 Support rugby player (4)

Sudoku

Fill in the squares in the grid so that every row, column and each of the nine 3x3 squares contain all the digits from one to nine.

MEDIUM GRID

7			4					
	4	9		3			6	
1						9		
	3				7	2		1
			9		8			
5		2	3				7	
		4						9
	6			5		3	1	
					6			8

HARD GRID

	5		2			3		
				5			9	
8					7		2	
7		2			5			4
	6						7	
4			9			1		5
	8		7					9
	1			8				
		4			6		5	

Were you right? Turn to page 182 for the answers

The butterfly

Charlie finds how one small event can have such an unpredictable

When Charlie Copford stepped off the pavement to avoid bumping into an old lady, he gave no thought to the Brazilian butterfly. A passing car was about to hit him when a man appeared from nowhere and barged Charlie back up the kerb.

He came to in a hospital bed with WPC Rosemary McKay at his side. She explained that it was she who had called an ambulance, taken names and addresses of witnesses, searched his wallet and phoned his employer. She had also visited his flat and learned from neighbours that there was no wife and his next of kin, his mother, lived in New Zealand.

After that, she dozed by his bedside until he came round.

"Amazing," said Charlie. "One minute I'm off to work. The next thing I know is waking up here."

"It's a pity you don't remember. Three witnesses say they saw you step into the road and were about to be run over when a man threw himself at you, pushing you on to the pavement where you banged your head. He was tall, dressed in a grey suit with a pink shirt."

"Sounds like he saved my life. He's a hero. Can you find him?"

"He appeared from nowhere, then vanished. I think he was your guardian angel, Charlie." Rosemary laughed. "Now, listen. I'm going off duty. Anything you'd like me to do for you? Phone anyone? Girlfriend, perhaps?"

"Don't have one," Charlie said. "How about you?"

Rosemary blushed. "I'm not sure that's relevant, Mr Copford, but since you ask, there's no man in my life at the moment."

"Perhaps, there's room for me, then?"

She smiled: "We'll see. I'll try to look in tonight."

Charlie drifted off to sleep and woke to the sound of footsteps. He could see a figure through the glass panel in the door. Suddenly, without the door opening, a tall man was inside the room. Ordinary men do not walk through closed doors, Charlie thought. The stranger was wearing a grey suit and a pink shirt. He watched, fascinated, as the man walked towards him, passing through two beds and a table. That was the sort of thing a ghost would do. Charlie didn't believe in ghosts and felt no fear. What's more, he fitted the description of the man who'd saved his life. "Hi, Charlie," said the stranger. "Guess I shoved you too hard. I'm sorry."

"Don't apologise. I'd have been a goner," Charlie said. "It's kind of you to visit me, Mr... er?"

"Rodney Angel."

"Well, Rodney, you saved my life."

"That's my job. I'm a BIA - Brazilian Intervening Angel. The name comes from the belief that a butterfly flapping its wings in Brazil..."

"Hold on. Yes, I know all about the butterfly effect but - are you saying you're a... a...?"

"Yes, Charlie. I'm an angel."

Charlie let that sink in, slowly. "You don't look like one, Rodney."

"That's the idea. We wear clothing suitable to the mission."

"Blimey," Charlie gazed at Rodney in awe. "But why me?"

"It would be impossible to rescue everyone on the planet who dies before their time is up. Think of all the disasters. Our resources are limited."

> **"It would be impossible to rescue everyone on the planet who dies before their time is up. Think of all the disasters"**

"So how come I was picked?"

Rodney sighed. "You weren't. My mission was to protect an Afghan philanthropist who has been working to eliminate poppy growing and drug trafficking in his own country. Still with me?"

Charlie nodded.

"This man was in a chauffeur-driven car on his way to Heathrow when the driver got into an argument with his wife on his mobile. Because he was distracted, he would have hit you and killed you. This would have meant that the policewoman would have detained the chauffeur and his passenger to take statements. As a result, our man would have missed his plane and wouldn't have attended a vital meeting that could

Words Bill Meehan / Illustration Kate Davies

effect

esult

help eliminate drug trafficking."

"You couldn't have had much warning," Charlie said.

"Milliseconds only," said Rodney. "But it's goodbye now, Charlie. I'm on standby."

"Hang on," Charlie protested. "You can't just go off. I want to know what happens next."

"You get discharged from hospital with no after-effects. You go back to work. Now I must go."

"And who gets the girl?"

Rodney looked anxious. "I can't tell you that. We operate on a need-to-know basis."

"Well, thanks all the same. Take care, Rodney."

"You're the one who must take care, Charlie. I'm immortal."

He walked straight through the bedside locker without a backward glance.

That evening, Rosemary arrived. She looked beautiful, wearing a red dress and bearing gifts of grapes and chocolates.

"Charlie, you look as though you've seen a ghost."

"I've been asleep. Think I've been dreaming."

"Sleep is exactly what you need. The doc says you'll be discharged tomorrow."

"Rosemary, do you know the theory of how a butterfly flapping its wings in Brazil starts a chain of events?"

"Of course. Like how that tall chap barged you back on to the pavement and saved your life, then I arrive to investigate and here we are together." She took Charlie's hand in hers and they sat gazing into each other's eyes.

"Rosemary, have you ever seen an angel?"

"Don't be silly, Charlie. Here, have a chocolate."

First, rake down

Writer Valery McConnell and **Yours** *readers remember the pleasures and perils of making a coal fire*

It was messy, time-consuming, and could be dangerous, but the result was magical. I'm talking about making a coal-fire. In the days before central heating, whatever your age, you had some hand in getting that fire going. So let's remember one of the great vanished rituals...

"As soon as I'd get in from school," writes **Ms E Jones**, "I would rake down the ashes, then tip them into a bucket – often the dust would fly around, creating another job. Next I'd roll up some paper..." It seems a whole generation of British children spent their evenings making elaborate firelighters from old newspaper.

Shirley Balmforth emailed, "Broadsheets made the best ones. You began by folding a sheet of newspaper diagonally, then folding in small strips over and over until you had a long flat strip. This was then made into a v-shape and criss-crossed until you had a concertina shape which was finished off with a twist at the top to stop it unravelling."

Back to Ms Jones' fire... "I'd place the paper rolls on the cinders and stack up a few sticks of wood. Some small lumps of coal would follow and then I'd strike a match and light the paper.

"Hopefully it would get going straightaway. There would be a crackle from the wood and soon a lovely glow. If not, then a big sigh, grab a big sheet of paper and hold it across for the fire to draw."

Doreen Hopwood's family had an interesting variation. "We had a gas cooker with a long rubber hose attached and a gas poker on the other end. We would light it in the kitchen and either Dad or Mum would walk through the house to the lounge and push the flaming poker into the coals to get them going. Can you imagine how people would react today to this highly dangerous practice?"

Back then, of course, there were more 'highly dangerous practices' going on than you could shake a stick at... Remember this one?

"We regularly had a coal fire in the back room, only using the front room on a Sunday," says **Sue Thorp**. "Instead of lighting the fire in there from scratch, Dad used a shovel to take half the burning coals from the back room to the front! All this with four children under eight being told to keep well out of the way."

Joan Brown's mum was the dare-devil, "To give our coal oven a good clean, come November time she would light a banger and throw it under the oven with great results - after the clean up!"

While **Mrs Hay** explained, "My parents had a black lead grate with an over mantel.

Around the mantel was a piece of curtain wire, for airing clothes. One of my earliest memories is sitting in my pram and watching a nappy start to scorch. The room filled with smoke and my mother had to rescue me."

No wonder so many of you had a visit from the Fire Brigade, including Lyn Lewis. "I got back from school one day to find a fire engine outside our house. My mum had thrown a bowl of spilt sugar on the lit fire which then set the chimney on fire!"

Jan McPherson was coming home from Sunday school when she saw firemen with hoses outside her house. "Mum had put the fat from the Sunday joint on to the fire to light it and the paper had caught alight and the chimney was on fire. No Sunday roast and we spent the afternoon cleaning."

It wasn't sugar or fat that fanned the flames for **Mrs Taylor**... "I was ten, my brother was 12 and as our mother had an afternoon job we lit the fire when we came home from school. It was all laid out, so should have been simple.

"But one day it would not light and it was so cold my brother decided to go to the shed and get the paraffin can. We sprinkled it all over and threw the match on. It went 'poof!' and singed my hair and eyebrows and my brother burnt his school jumper all down the front. We rushed into the kitchen for

the ashes

PICS: GETTY

There were some dangerous moments but nothing could beat the welcome glow of a real fire.

water and put the fire out, then sat quivering on the floor until Mother came home. Boy did we get a good hiding."

It wasn't always what went up the chimney that was a problem. "One night, I was bathing baby Melanie in front of the fire," writes **Jennifer Hall**.

"Suddenly there was a rumble and soot fell in the bath and all over the poor baby. Then a bird missed the fire by inches and flew up and flapped on the ceiling, leaving soot everywhere before landing in the baby's pram. I was horrified. I wrapped Melanie in a blanket, popped her

into a highchair and asked my four-year-old daughter, Laura, to hold on to her. I flung another blanket over the bird. Going outside for help I asked a group of lads to fetch my husband who was working a street away. He hurried back and order was eventually restored!"

Messy and sometimes dangerous, but as **Pat Crick** emailed: "Central heating may be a lot cleaner, but an open fire, a living flame, is like a friend." And we reap such wonderful memories.

The Christmas

George's request sets Mary dreaming impossible dreams...

Mary was stirring the Christmas pudding when George bellowed: "What do you want for Christmas this year?" As he breezed through the kitchen en-route to the garage, he barely stopped for her answer, so intent was he on some vital DIY job or other.

Mary considered the question. "I don't really know," she said, trying to think of some useful article that George could be trusted to buy.

"Write me a list," he shouted over his shoulder.

"Righto," replied Mary, but her voice was drowned out by the door banging shut. She shrugged resignedly, used to George's abrupt ways. He was always busy on some practical task but a good man, nevertheless. Not one to buy you flowers, but handy if you wanted a dripping tap fixed.

She resumed stirring, but her mind was elsewhere. What should she ask for? Some bubble bath? Not the cheap stuff with bubbles that disappeared too quickly. Something fragrant and expensive. She smiled as she imagined herself in a steam-filled bathroom, lying back in a haze of scented foam, sipping delicately from a Champagne flute. It wasn't the bubble bath she craved so much as the chance to be pampered like a film star. She shook herself out of the reverie and bustled over to the cupboard to fetch a bag of currants.

Seeing her shopping notepad pinned to the door, she tore off a sheet. After rummaging in the drawer for a pencil, she wrote Mary's Xmas List across the top with a squiggly line underneath. Then she put a number one and scrawled Bubble Bath next to it.

Taking out the scales, she weighed the currants and tipped them into a bowl. She had followed the recipe so many times that she didn't have to concentrate. Instead, her mind continued to dwell on the thorny issue of her present list. If she was going to be self-indulgent, she could do with a new mirror. Her old one was cracked, making it difficult to see her reflection properly. Mind you, at her age did she want to see her reflection properly? Perhaps, it was best to stay blissfully ignorant of the lines that now adorned her face.

grabbed the pencil and wrote A Hand Mirror next to number two in the margin.

The sultanas followed the currants into the mixture and, as she started to stir, Mary's mind wandered again. What else did she need? The sound of rain against the window brought George to mind – that would put paid to his DIY activities. It also reminded her that she needed a new umbrella. Her black one had a broken spoke and looked like a lopsided old crow. Maybe she could ask for a pink one this time? That would brighten winter's depressing rainy days.

As she added Umbrella to her list, she thought wistfully it would be nice if the umbrella could also be a magic one – one that protected you from

---

What she'd really like would be a magic mirror. One that didn't reflect her present image, but somehow showed the past. It would show her aged 20, when she'd first met George

---

What she'd really like would be a magic mirror. One that didn't reflect her present image, but somehow showed the past. It would show her aged 20, when she'd first met George. Her skin had been smooth then, with a hint of rose in her cheeks. Her eyes had been big and bright – now they looked more like the currants she'd put in the pudding.

Mary started: the pudding! She must get on, or there wouldn't be time to steam it. Fetching the sultanas, she caught sight of the list. She

life's misfortunes as well as the rain. She wished she'd had such a thing when her beloved parents passed away or on the day George had been made redundant...

The list was almost long enough. George quickly got bored if he had to spend too long at the shops. Also, they were trying to keep the cost of Christmas down now they were retired. Pencil poised, she tried to think of one more inexpensive item. Hmm. It occurred to her that a photo

wish list

album would be useful. Her daughter, Julie, was always sending snaps of the grandchildren, Jamie and Becky, and one of Mary's favourite occupations was leafing through old family albums remembering the happy times; holidays, birthday parties and past Christmases.

Wouldn't it be wonderful if she could have an album with snaps of the future in it? Would Jamie become a famous footballer? Would Becky one day be a glowing bride? She imagined her young granddaughter in a fairytale dress beaming at the side of a lovely young man. Who else would be in the photo? Their parents, of course. And please, please could she and George be there too? She reached for her list and wrote Photo Album.

The pudding was ready. Mary poured the mixture into a bowl and tied the greaseproof paper firmly over it as she had so many times before. She set it in the steamer over a pan of water, then went upstairs to tidy herself up.

The rain had indeed driven George indoors. He marched into the kitchen, then stopped as he saw Mary's list lying on the worktop. He glanced at it quickly: bubble bath, a mirror, an umbrella and a photo album. That shouldn't be too difficult, he thought, a quick trip into town should do it. Nothing too expensive or impractical. Good old down-to-earth Mary. She didn't ask for much.

But she did in her dreams, George. She did in her dreams.

Puzzle answers

PAGE 150

Two-speed crossword

ACROSS: 1 Mutate, 4 Colossal, 10 Detergent, 11 Franc, 12 Ruled, 13 Spotlight, 14 Tragedy, 16 Estate, 19 Whisky, 21 Siberia, 23 Scoundrel, 25 Elgar, 27 Cling, 28 Attracted, 29 Overtime, 30 Stupor.

DOWN: 1 Moderate, 2 Total, 3 Tiredness, 5 Outcome, 6 Offal, 7 Slaughter, 8 Locate, 9 Jersey, 15 Aphrodite, 17 Table salt, 18 Labrador, 20 Yardarm, 21 Salute, 22 Psycho, 24 Night, 26 Get up.

Medium Sudoku

1	9	6	7	5	2	4	8	3
7	8	4	1	6	3	9	5	2
3	5	2	8	4	9	6	7	1
4	7	3	2	9	8	1	6	5
6	1	9	4	7	5	2	3	8
5	2	8	3	1	6	7	4	9
9	3	7	5	2	4	8	1	6
2	4	5	6	8	1	3	9	7
8	6	1	9	3	7	5	2	4

Hard Sudoku

1	9	8	3	2	5	7	6	4
6	4	3	1	7	8	9	2	5
7	2	5	9	6	4	3	1	8
5	7	2	8	4	9	6	3	1
4	6	9	2	1	3	8	5	7
3	8	1	7	5	6	4	9	2
8	5	4	6	3	2	1	7	9
2	3	7	4	9	1	5	8	6
9	1	6	5	8	7	2	4	3

PAGE 158

Two-speed crossword

ACROSS: 8 Handsome, 9 Untie, 10 Etna, 11 Ghost, 12 Tory, 13 Pitch, 14 Ostracise, 16 Odour, 17 Mural, 22 Nightclub, 24 Stalk, 26 Beam, 27 Bobby, 28 Leek, 29 Magic, 30 European.

DOWN: 1 Captain, 2 Advanced, 3 Gorge, 4 Remorse, 5 Buttercup, 6 Static, 7 Repress, 15 Hunchback, 18 Antelope, 19 Dilemma, 20 Tumbler, 21 Illegal, 23 Homage, 25 Lycra.

Medium Sudoku

7	1	9	8	5	4	3	6	2
4	5	8	6	2	3	7	9	1
2	3	6	1	9	7	4	5	8
6	9	7	5	1	2	8	4	3
5	2	3	7	4	8	9	1	6
1	8	4	9	3	6	2	7	5
9	4	1	3	8	5	6	2	7
8	7	5	2	6	9	1	3	4
3	6	2	4	7	1	5	8	9

Hard Sudoku

4	8	5	9	2	6	3	7	1
7	9	6	8	3	1	5	2	4
3	1	2	4	5	7	6	9	8
2	6	7	1	4	3	8	5	9
8	4	3	6	9	5	2	1	7
1	5	9	7	8	2	4	3	6
5	7	8	2	1	4	9	6	3
6	3	4	5	7	9	1	8	2
9	2	1	3	6	8	7	4	5

PAGE 166

Two-speed crossword

ACROSS: 3 Newsreader, 8 Nepali, 9 Alarmist, 10 Snapshot, 11 Closed, 12 Embraced, 15 Middle-of-the-road, 17 Composer, 19 Needle, 23 Cable car, 24 Tasmania, 25 Reeled, 26 Institutes.

DOWN: 1 Kennel, 2 Pampas, 3 Nightdress, 4 Weather forecast, 5 Rear, 6 Armchair, 7 Ensure, 11 Comic, 13 Behind bars, 14 Dodge, 16 Diplomat, 18 Obtain, 20 Eleven, 21 Leaves, 22 Knot.

Medium Sudoku

1	4	9	3	7	5	6	2	8
7	5	2	6	1	8	3	4	9
6	8	3	9	2	4	1	5	7
4	7	6	2	5	3	9	8	1
2	3	5	8	9	1	4	7	6
8	9	1	7	4	6	2	3	5
9	1	4	5	8	2	7	6	3
5	6	7	4	3	9	8	1	2
3	2	8	1	6	7	5	9	4

Hard Sudoku

9	2	6	3	5	8	1	7	4
7	4	5	6	2	1	9	8	3
8	1	3	4	7	9	2	5	6
1	7	9	5	6	3	8	4	2
4	3	2	9	8	7	6	1	5
5	6	8	1	4	2	7	3	9
3	8	7	2	9	5	4	6	1
2	5	4	7	1	6	3	9	8
6	9	1	8	3	4	5	2	7

PAGE 174

Two-speed crossword

ACROSS: 1 Grease, 4 Producer, 8 Liberate, 9 Cagney, 10 Date, 11 Grateful, 14 Readies, 16 Apparel, 18 Affairs, 20 Masters, 22 Electric, 24 Cape, 26 Depend, 27 Thriller, 28 Nuthatch, 29 Entrap.

DOWN: 1 Gold, 2 Alexandra, 3 Erase, 4 Pledge, 5 Draft, 6 Conifer, 7 Royal flush, 12 Alpha, 13 Armageddon, 15 Error, 17 Autopilot, 19 Fleapit, 21 Scotch, 23 Tonga, 24 Carve, 25 Prop.

Medium Sudoku

7	5	6	4	8	9	1	2	3
8	4	9	1	3	2	5	6	7
1	2	3	6	7	5	9	8	4
4	3	8	5	6	7	2	9	1
6	7	1	9	2	8	4	3	5
5	9	2	3	4	1	8	7	6
2	8	4	7	1	3	6	5	9
9	6	7	8	5	4	3	1	2
3	1	5	2	9	6	7	4	8

Hard Sudoku

6	5	9	2	4	1	3	8	7
1	2	7	8	5	3	4	9	6
8	4	3	6	9	7	5	2	1
7	9	2	1	6	5	8	3	4
5	6	1	4	3	8	9	7	2
4	3	8	9	7	2	1	6	5
3	8	5	7	2	4	6	1	9
2	1	6	5	8	9	7	4	3
9	7	4	3	1	6	2	5	8